"A wonderful reference. Organized, informative and very inspiring—makes you want to get out there and create something!"

—STUART A. GOLDMAN, The Stuart Goldman Company

"Forsher's book is a necessary tool for all of you documentary filmmakers, beginning and experienced alike ... plus any fiction filmmaker in need of using historical footage or images."

—LEITH ADAMS, retired Warner Bros. Corporate Archivist

"Provides a comprehensive and accessible introduction to a wide range of audio visual materials, and will be exceptionally useful for media story-tellers. A roadmap about how to find and use these treasures."

—STEPHEN MCDOWELL, John H. Phipps Professor of Communication, Florida State University

"Clear and comprehensive, *Stock Footage* is an absolutely essential resource for all who make documentary and scripted films."

—DIANE CARSON, past president, University Film and Video Association; producer/director, *Other People's Footage: Copyright & Fair Use*

"An informative, engaging book that tells you everything you need to know about the subject, from what to look for, how to find it, and equally important, how to negotiate the best deal for using it. A must-have resource for filmmakers."

—CAROLE KIRSCHNER, author, *Hollywood Game Plan*

"From an expert who loves the subject, *Stock Footage and Everything Under the Sun* is more than an essential filmmaking handbook, offering fresh and creative approaches to accessing and legally using archival materials."

—BETSY A. MCLANE, Director Emerita IDA, author of *A New History of Documentary Film*

"Likely to become required reading for independent filmmakers as well as those within organizations, non-profits and other entities whose mandate is to make films happen at low cost, but without sacrificing quality of acquired materials."

—MICHAEL TOBIAS, author, filmmaker

"Well structured—and a good reference to have on your shelf!"

—ROBERT JOHNSON, JR., Framingham State University

"*Stock Footage* provides a treasure trove of information on archival material. Now I know what to do with the outtakes that I shot of Andy Warhol back in 1971. Hallelujah that this book now exists as a precautionary tale for others!"

—ALEXIS KRASILOVSKY, writer/director, *Women Behind the Camera*, professor, Dept. of Cinema and Television Arts, California State University, Northridge

"As a filmmaker who has made documentaries in the past, I wish I'd had this book years ago as a guide for how to get started. *Stock Footage* is sure to become an indispensable book to add to any filmmaker's collection."

—ERIN CORRADO, One Movie, Our Views

USING ARCHIVAL MATERIAL TO MAKE

STOCK FOOTAGE

+ everything under the sun

YOUR GOOD FILM GREAT

James Forsher

MICHAEL WIESE PRODUCTIONS

Published by Michael Wiese Productions
12400 Ventura Blvd. #1111
Studio City, CA 91604
(818) 379-8799, (818) 986-3408 (FAX)
mw@mwp.com
www.mwp.com

Cover design by Johnny Ink. www.johnnyink.com
Interior design by William Morosi
Copyediting by David Wright
Printed by McNaughton & Gunn

Manufactured in the United States of America

Names: Forsher, James, 1953-
Title: Stock footage + everything under the sun : using archival material to
  make your good film great / James Forsher.
Other titles: Stock footage plus everything under the sun
Description: Studio City, CA : Michael Wiese Productions, [2019]
Identifiers: LCCN 2018022885 | ISBN 9781615932955
Subjects: LCSH: Stock footage. | Archival materials. | Motion
  pictures--Production and direction. | Television--Production and direction.
Classification: LCC PN1995.9.S6964 F67 2019 | DDC 025.17/73--dc23
LC record available at https://lccn.loc.gov/2018022885

To my wife, Neena, and daughter, Lily, for their patience and understanding while I researched and wrote this book.

CONTENTS

PART ONE

WHAT TO LOOK FOR

ACKNOWLEDGMENTS

This guide to archival material began when I was a kid. My mom and her producing partner, Adolph Zukor 2nd, were developing projects at Paramount Studios and decided I should not only see the lot, but understand what was going on there. That meant being left at the set of *Bonanza* and watched over by grips as they took meetings or watching the first year of *Star Trek* being shot. This started a lifelong love affair with Hollywood.

When I was finishing college, my mom and Adolph gave me the best graduation present, an interview with Adolph Zukor, the founder of Paramount . . . and suggested I try to make a film centered on the interview. That got me excited about making films.

Ever since then, my career has only lasted with the help of many patient and kindhearted mentors. My first feature film, *Ticket to Hollywood*, came about because studio executive Jonathan Dana took a chance and funded and distributed the film. Later, producer Stan Caidin stepped up and negotiated financing and output deals for my next three features.

Many years later, I realized that I wished someone would have written a guide for finding the elements we put into our films, something that took me a couple of decades to learn. This book would not exist if Michael Wiese and Ken Lee at Michael Wiese Productions didn't take a chance—just like my earlier mentors— at an unproven but interesting idea. Many thanks for their trust.

In writing this book, many of my colleagues over the years stepped forward to help. The late Eric Caidin, one of the great movie poster collectors and grindhouse aficionados, generously helped during the early stages of my research. My old producing partner Marc Wanamaker, owner of Bison Archives, has generously given advice and images over the years. Former Warner Bros. archivist Leith Adams also contributed a lot of wisdom about the meaning of what an archive can bring to a project.

I also must thank film archivists Michael Yakaitis and Wayne Blankenship who at different times ran my film archive. They kept it organized and allowed the footage we collected to be used by clients around the world for nearly two decades.

In writing this book, I had a large number of advisors that I want to thank; without their help the book could never have been finished. These include film clip licensing gurus James Tumminia and Lisa Kane, researcher extraordinaire Bonnie Rowan, documentary filmmakers Ally Acker and Stuart Goldman, Footage.net's David Seevers, and my archival representative, Jessica Berman of Global ImageWorks.

INTRODUCTION

When many filmmakers hear the term "archival" they immediately think of old black-and-white motion pictures, scratchy newsreels, educational films or classic TV shows. That is only one very small part of the equation.

Actually, archival material constitutes everything that has been created up to the second you are reading this introduction. Everything. Films, TV shows, webisodes, print ads. Posters. Music. Everything. It may seem counter-intuitive, but it has nothing to do with being old.

That's right. Just like everything in our lives, archival material is all the material that falls into the past tense. One second old. One hour old. One hundred thousand years old. It's archival material.

Stock Footage + Everything Else Under the Sun is your guidebook to unleashing your power of finding and using archival material in helping you tell the best, most powerful and interesting story.

Both fiction and non-fiction programs may all start with the same common denominator, a desire to tell a story about factual events, but the filmmaker has a choice of *how* they are going to tell that story. Will it exist only in the present tense, or will they create a story that integrates a contemporary narrative with a storyline that ties in the past? The key ingredient in this form of creating entertainment is the use of archival elements.

This book was inspired by my forty-year-long love affair with finding and using archival material in film productions. My own relationship with archival material goes back to the very first film I produced back in the late 1970s. I was given an interview with film pioneer Adolph Zukor, founder of Paramount Studios and the first person to bring a feature film to America. Zukor told an amazing story, but he was ninety-five years old at the time of the interview and I needed a lot of visuals to help bring his story to life.

And that is when I discovered the incredible world of archival material. The show I was producing was going to require motion pictures, newsreels, stills, old music and documents from the years 1890 to 1930. I began hunting and that led me to the underground world of archival material collectors.

I sat through hours of viewing films, sifted through thousands of still pictures and heard countless stories from the men and women who had a passion about classic Hollywood and were determined to help preserve its memories.

I learned the art of negotiating very different deals, hand-holding collectors who were reticent to let go of their precious material, as well as convincing old film stars and producers to allow me to interview them about their experiences working at Paramount Studios for my show. Once I was finished with the Adolph Zukor documentary, I realized that making a film was much more interesting when it entailed adding a true detective hunt to find the real story. I would be hooked for the rest of my life.

If you need something that looks contemporary, you will hunt for archival material that looks like it was shot recently. However, if you are looking for material that establishes a time period, older archival material fits the bill. The great advantage of all this material is that it quickly establishes exactly at what time your story takes place, where it takes place and the environment it takes place in. It can take us back a week or centuries. It is one of the greatest tools filmmakers have available to them.

And it's environmentally friendly. Archival films and print material are recycled material. It was created for any of a number of purposes, and luckily not thrown away. This includes feature films, feature film outtakes, newsreels, cartoons, industrial films, home movies, corporate films and all manners of printed material. You get the idea. If it was preserved, it is archival.

What do feature films like *Hugo, Back to the Future Part II*, or *Star Trek Generations* all share in common? They all used archival material. Films like these have proven that archival material is not limited for use in documentaries and helps make a filmmaker's story come to life.

HOW TO USE THIS BOOK

This is the book I wish I had been able to read when I first started producing films many years ago.

I would like to have read a thorough guide that explored the way of thinking and organizing my material (and my thoughts) as I pieced together the complex jigsaw puzzle that is a film project.

I want you to use this book in the same way—as a lifelong resource to help you think, organize and create.

Whether a novice or an old pro, archival material hunters all share the same game plan when starting their hunt. In short, it goes like this:

- Research the topic. Find out everything you can about its history, people and institutions involved.
- Identify what material *might* work in your project.
- Create a list of sources where the items might be found.
- Contact these places and try to get copies of the material.
- Update this process with new leads and start all over again.
- See if the material you have accessed works in your creative project.
- Negotiate the right to use it or get legal proof it is in the public domain.

Using this game plan, the following pages take you step-by-step through the journey of finding and accessing material for your project.

The book is broken up into four parts. Each part serves as both an overview of the steps involved and as a reference guide with contact information that can lead you to valuable collections, websites, books and interviews with experts who work in archival material on a daily basis.

Part One explores the most common archival elements that go into a film or television show. This include movies, television shows, music, animated elements, print elements and official documents. Each chapter gives a brief history of the technology, and how that technology has evolved.

Part Two looks at where the archival material is and how to access it. We look at the different locations that hold large motion picture collections, TV shows, commercials, music, graphics, news, etc.

Part Three explores the search process; how to actually find the material you might need. It gives you the basic information to accomplish the fundamental steps of researching the materials you are going to be looking for. It takes you into the world of "clearing archival material." Finding it is step one, finding out if you can legally use it is the next step. Then you need to find out about who the real owner is and how much money they want. It is also the step in which you might discover that the material is actually in the "public domain" and you can use it without paying a copyright fee.

Part Three also explores the art of negotiating deals. Archival material might not cost anything. Then again, it might cost thirty thousand dollars a minute. You need to know what options you have as a negotiator, trying to get the best price but not wanting to bargain to the point that your seller calls off the deal because they can't put up with you. We review all of the final steps to make sure you have done it all right. For example, have you made sure you have all the legal protection you will need, which means possibly getting Errors & Omissions insurance? This is a policy that ensures that if you are sued you have insurance covering you.

Part Four examines how you can benefit from making money yourself from archival materials you might own. This may include material you have shot, old movies you inherited or print collections you have assembled. It is all worth something to somebody.

The book is both a guide and a resource book. Reading the entire book will give you a broad overview of how to conduct your search. For those needing specific advice, chapters can serve as a reference guide. Each chapter has a detailed overview of the topic, company names and internet sites. Either way, you will unlock a world of treasures to put into your media project, much of it free for the taking.

You should find it helpful in getting you started on your first serious hunt for archival material. It should also be equally helpful in several years when you have done the hunt a few times but need to find an obscure website I mentioned and that linked you to the perfect collection for your project.

Please note: this book is not intended to provide any methods, justification, or excuses for any illegal action that violates the rights of anyone possessing material you want to use. This book gives you an overview of the world of archival material, but as I stress throughout the book, you need to protect yourself—and be fair to others--by making the right ethical and legal decisions.

PART 1

WHAT TO LOOK FOR

CHAPTER 1

SHORT FILMS

- **Type of medium:** Film, 1894 to late 1990s.
- **Years in use:** 1894 to the present.
- **Audience:** Theatrical, internet.
- **US copyright status:** Pre-1920 are in public domain. Post-1920, mix of public domain and copyright. Post-1976, copyright for 75 years from date of authorship.

FIGURE 1.1. *Little Rascals* poster. Forsher Collection.

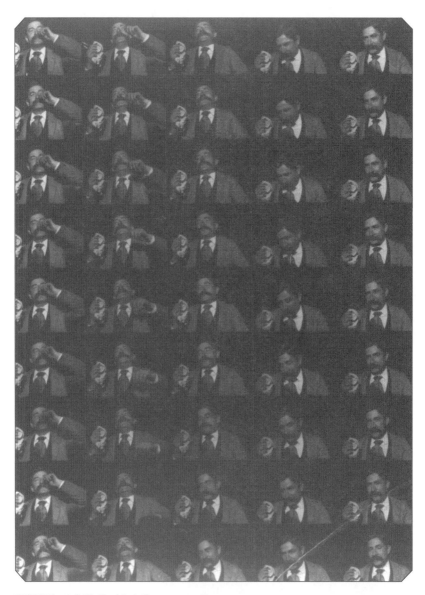

FIGURE 1.2. Still: *Fred Ott's Sneeze.* 1894. Footagesource.com

☙ INTRODUCTION

One of the most requested forms of archival media is film-based "shorts"—films lasting up to a half hour in length. These were the first moving pictures ever made. We are lucky that thousands of these films have survived the years, many going back to the mid-1890s, shot in every region of the world.

1890s—IT STARTED WITH A SNEEZE

The motion picture began as an experiment when filmmakers realized that playing still images very quickly gave the illusion of movement. Thomas Edison was one of the first to capitalize on this invention, filming his worker Fred Ott sneezing back in January, 1894. Edison and others soon created hand-cranked motion picture cameras and showed their films on machines like Edison's kinetoscope at his penny arcades. This was the birth of motion pictures.

In Europe, pioneer filmmakers Auguste and Louis Lumière began their career in the 1890s by shooting events on the streets and at

FIGURE 1.3. Lumière brothers. *Arrival of a Train*, 1896. Footagesource.com

FIGURE 1.4. Nickelodeon Theater. Pittsburgh, PA, circa 1905. Forsher Collection.

public meeting places in Paris, France. They recorded people going to work, a train arriving or a family strolling. These images became the subject of their programs that would find their way onto their cinematographe projection device or be seen in penny arcade peep devices around the world.

Many other filmmakers soon joined in and started creating early silent films, sometimes called *actualities*. They serve as a record of various real-life events happening over a decade from different parts of the world. The films reflected the values and social makeup of the time, often showing the attitude of society toward racism, sexism and religious intolerance. Today, these films developed a secondary value. For the first time in history we were able to record the lifestyle of a fixed period that has all but disappeared.

In 1905 the "nickel theater" opened in Pittsburgh, PA. The idea was novel at the time; have an audience come into an auditorium and project for them an hour's worth of short films, have a piano play some music and charge them a nickel. Repeat this each hour and you are making some serious money.

The Nickelodeon became an overnight hit, and the nickel theater concept spread around the country. Within a year, several thousand theaters had sprung up around the United States and filmmakers had a new venue for selling their short films. It also allowed nickel theater owners to get around Edison's copyrights and patent police by buying foreign projectors and purchasing foreign-made films or those made by independent filmmakers in the United States.

FIGURE 1.5. *Great Train Robbery*, 1903. Library of Congress.

It was during this time that one film was made that would change motion pictures forever; the first "narrative" film was produced. In 1903, Edwin S. Porter produced *The Great Train Robbery*. Though it was only a few minutes long, it was a true action-adventure film with a story line featuring train robbers holding up a train and their pursuit by law enforcement. Audiences were entertained and their expectations of what film could deliver was suddenly lifted to new heights.

1920s–1950s

With the growing popularity of film theaters and the feature film, shorts were added to the programs. Studios began producing short programs to accompany features, offering a wide variety of topics.

LAUREL AND HARDY

Producer Hal Roach matched Stan Laurel and Oliver Hardy as a comedy team back in the late 1920s, and for the next two decades they created dozens of short comedies that have entertained audiences to this day.

FIGURE 1.6. Laurel and Hardy from short educational film on plastics. Footagesource.com

THE THREE STOOGES

Columbia Studios, a relatively small studio during the 1930s, created a niche for themselves with the comedy team of The Three Stooges. Beginning as sidekicks to comedian Ted Healy, they soon discovered they were better off without him and went on to star in roughly 190 films over the next two decades.

LITTLE RASCALS

Hal Roach produced a variety of other shorts with stars such as Will Rogers and Harold Lloyd, but he found no greater success than with that of a group of kids whose first silent shorts came out in the mid 1920s. First called the "Our Gang" comedies and eventually renamed the "Little Rascals," they featured three generations of kids growing up on the screen with such legendary talent as Alfalfa, Spanky and Darla.

PETE SMITH SPECIALTIES

MGM produced a series of shorts to accompany their features. One series still seen on TCM is the Pete Smith specialties, in which narrator Pete Smith would show the humor in everyday subjects. Other MGM shorts included James Fitzpatrick's *Traveltalks*, one of the earliest travel series ever produced.

SERIALS

Studios like Mascot and Republic found their niche in producing Saturday morning serials. These were ten- or twenty-minute programs that were part of a series, each ending with a "cliff-hanger" in which the hero or heroine faced what appeared to be certain death. To see how the hero or heroine would survive you had to return to the theater the following week. These became incredibly popular during the Depression and World War II, and were the vehicles that launched the careers of such legendary stars as John Wayne to show off their talent.

FIGURE 1.7. *Rin Tin Tin Jr.* Mascot Pictures serial. Forsher Collection.

❦ SUMMARY

There is a reason archival film is the most popular form of archival material available. Hundreds of thousands of short films exist that explore almost every aspect of modern culture going back nearly 125 years. Fiction, non-fiction, cartoons, industrial age, corporate world. You name it and a film was done on it. They often featured legendary stars, famous locations and fantastic visuals.

The key for you—the filmmaker—is to see how archival material can help better tell your story. Don't self-censor as you write your outline structure. Let your research lead you to at least trying to integrate material that will make the difference between a somewhat watchable film and a truly entertaining and interesting one.

CHAPTER 2

FEATURE FILMS

- **Type of medium:** Film-based, 1912 to early 2000s.
- **Years in use:** 1893 to the present.
- **Audience:** Worldwide.
- **Copyright status:** Most films before 1920 are in the public domain. 1920 to 1976, films are a mixture of pubic domain and copyrighted. 1976 on, films are copyrighted between 50 and 75 years

FIGURE 2.1. *Queen Elizabeth* (1912). First feature-length film shown in America, starring Sarah Bernhardt. Footagesource.com

❧ INTRODUCTION

After several years of experimenting with making short films and showing them to audiences at nickel theaters, exhibitors began to wonder what could expand the movie-going experience. Nickel theater owner Adolph Zukor read about a French motion picture, *Queen Elizabeth*, that was over an hour in length, and he decided to see if American audiences had the patience to sit and watch a filmed play. He premiered the film in July, 1912, at the Lyceum Theatre in New York. It was a huge hit and within a year, exhibitors abandoned nickel theaters and began building what became "movie palaces." Because audiences now expected feature-length films to entertain them, several profound changes came to the motion picture industry over the following decades.

FIGURE 2.2. Premiere of Charlie Chaplin's *City Lights*. Finished during the early years of sound, Chaplin decided to continue producing in the silent film format with a musical score. Footagesource.com

❦ FEATURE FILMS WITH SOUND

Thomas Edison began to experiment with sound films in the early 1900s. However, it took over two decades for the technology of putting soundtracks on film to be developed. Newsreels and animated cartoons first tried synchronous sound in the mid 1920s. In 1928, Warner Bros. premiered *The Jazz Singer*, which featured mostly singing, but a few brief spoken lines were snuck in. Al Jolson uttered these few spoken words, "You ain't heard nothin' yet," and the silent-film era suddenly came to an end. Theaters around the country began installing sound systems, studios rebuilt their stages and by 1930 the sound film had taken over.

❦ COLOR

Filmmakers began hand-coloring their films at the beginning of the twentieth century, but it was expensive and time-consuming. In the mid-1920s, Technicolor Corporation showed off its color process in such films as Universal's *Phantom of the Opera*. By the 1930s major studios utilized the expensive process for their biggest films such as *The Wizard of Oz* and *Gone with the Wind*.

By the late 1950s the cost of shooting and creating color prints had come down in price and the majority of films soon began to be shot and released in color.

❦ WIDE-FORMAT PRESENTATION

With the introduction of commercial television in the late 1940s, studios realized they had to offer a greater film-going experience to draw audiences to the theater. One technology that most studios took advantage of was increasing the "format" of the screen size. As can be seen in Figure 2.3, film formats evolved from the standardized 35mm from the beginning of the twentieth century

FIGURE 2.3. Different aspect ratios of film. From top to bottom: 35mm, 16mm and 8mm. Footagesource.com

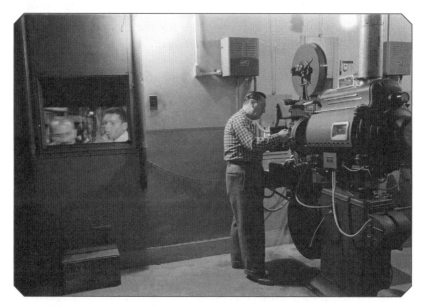

FIGURE 2.4. 35mm projection booth. Mid 1940s. Library of Congress.

to the early 1950s, when improved camera and projection systems allowed for systems like Panavision's 65mm and Cinerama's three-camera setup that offered audiences a screen as wide as the entire front of the theater. This was an expensive process and only a few films were completed using the Cinerama process, including *How the West Was Won*. Panavision offered a 70mm wide-angle presentation that offered a similar experience at a fraction of the cost.

In the early 1970s, IMAX corporation introduced the largest format film to date, a film that when projected filled an auditorium with an image several stories tall. To this day, IMAX stands as the ultimate in movie-going experience, and films like *Avatar, Star Wars, Star Trek* and *Black Panther* have been specially formatted to play at IMAX theaters.

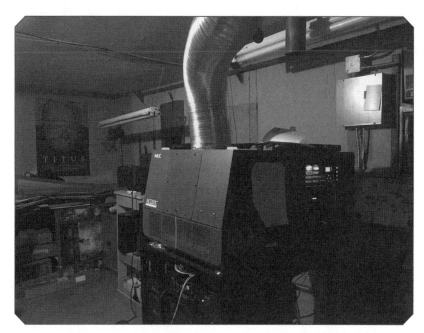

FIGURE 2.5. Digital projection booth. 2018. Courtesy of Faraway Entertainment.

ANALOG TO DIGITAL

In the early 2000s, the film industry moved away from emulsion-based film and began shooting and distributing all features as digital files projected by digital projectors. The era of film projection—after an entire century—had come to an end. Often times eBay lists classic projectors available for a fraction of their original cost . . . a great relic for anyone's media room.

SUMMARY

Feature films are expensive to produce. Over the years, it has taken tenacious producers, an army of skilled production personnel, and funding equivalent to raising massive buildings to create a modest-size feature film. If they are lucky, they make their money back in a relatively short period of time and then let it sit on a shelf.

But through the magic of licensing footage, you can get film clips from tens of thousands of feature films from all regions of the world for a very nominal price compared to their actual production costs. You can license a World War II battle, Armageddon-size disasters or legendary stars in their prime. You get the idea . . . a lot of bang for a *relatively* small amount of money. Note the stress on "relatively."

Just like shorts, when one designs the look and feel of a show, always remember what is potentially available to you and your budget.

The key to making sure a feature film fits your new production is to create a checklist that compares the film you might want to license to what you really need. Here is my suggested checklist:

Formatting: Is the format of your current production (hi def, maybe even 4K) going to work with 4:3 format?

Color or Black-and-White: How will you utilize black-and-white footage in your very colorful film?

Clothing: Does your narrative talk about a certain time and location? If so, do the clothes in the image fit that narrative? For example, if you are discussing America during World War II, will "flapper fashions" confuse the audience that knows those fashions came about in the early 1920s?

Cars: Will you be confusing your audience by putting in foreign cars in a US city when they weren't there originally? Or be talking about the 1940s but showing 1960 cars?

Transportation: Will you be showing Boeing 737 jets in the early 1950s? That may upset those that realize you are at least two decades off.

Use the same line of questioning for other elements in your footage, photos, music or artwork.

- Hair
- Language
- Communication
- Style of film
- Style of music

Finally, look at your budget and see if you have the funds available to license material. How much of your "profits" are you willing to never see for the film clip you want? These are important questions when anticipating—minimally—several thousand dollars a minute in licensing fees.

CHAPTER 3

NEWSREELS

- **Type of medium:** Film, 1898 to 1990. Video, 1990 to 2010. 2010 to the present, digital card capture.
- **Years in use:** 1898 to the present.
- **Audience:** Worldwide.
- **Copyright status:** 1896 to 1966. Mix of copyright and public domain. Contemporary newsreels are copyrighted.

FIGURE 3.1. *Hindenburg* exploding while landing. New Jersey, 1937. Footagesource.com

✿ INTRODUCTION

Penny arcades in the United States featured Edison's kinetoscope starting in 1893. These machines allowed viewers to look through a peephole and watch a short film. They became overnight sensations, with audiences standing around the block to see this technological wonder, but the novelty soon wore off. In 1898, a political event caught the attention of filmmakers, and taught them a lesson about drawing audiences. The US warship *Maine* was sunk in the harbor outside Havana. The United States declared war on Spain, and filmmakers began to satisfy the public's interest in the events by filming stories showing the war unfold.

A nationalistic fervor sent camera men shooting films showing US troops undergoing training exercises, Admiral Dewey taking a stroll on a ship and soldiers on horseback galloping off to fight a battle. The films were entertaining, yet ripe with propaganda. Devoid of

FIGURE 3.2. USS *Maine*, remains of the ship in Havana Harbor, 1898. Library of Congress.

any mention of Spain's perspective, the films reflected the United States at war, and as the Spanish-American War broke out, the newsreel had a chance to prove its power as a means of propagandizing the American role in the conflict. Titles defined America's propaganda message, such as J. Stuart Blackton's *Tearing Down the Spanish Flag* (1898), *Wreck of the Battleship Maine* (1898), *Filipinos Retreat from Trenches* (1899), or *Raising Old Glory over Morro Castle* (1899). The newsreel was born.

While some Americans were against the expansion of American possessions overseas and William Jennings Bryan planned on running for president as an anti-imperialist, the overall mood of the country grew to overwhelmingly support the war. The move toward foreign intervention grew along with the growth of cinema and they both served to fan each other. Audiences once again returned to the penny arcades to witness scenes of the war and see our troops in action. Few cared that many of the images they saw were recreated and didn't reflect the reality of the battles that were taking place.

The Spanish-American War was a natural vehicle to try to develop the powers of motion pictures in creating messages, and its comparatively naïve images allow us today to understand the propagandistic efforts made by the producers of the day. Thomas Edison, the most powerful studio head during the first decade of film production, realized that audiences wanted to see material that was interesting and entertaining.

❧ NEWSREELS CAPTURED THE EVENTS OF A MODERN WORLD

Thousands of newsreels would follow the Spanish-American War, and many had messages that were equally powerful. The San Francisco earthquake had filmmakers recording the damage to the city. Topsy the elephant was electrocuted in 1903 and became the

FIGURE 3.3. San Francisco earthquake. 1906. Footagesource.com

FIGURE 3.4. Electrocution of Topsy. 1903. Library of Congress.

FIGURE 3.5. Coronation of Nicholas II. 1896. Library of Congress.

subject of a sensational newsreel. *Beheading the Chinese Prisoner* (Lubin Studios, 1900) featured Caucasian actors portraying Chinese and reenacting the Boxer Rebellion, falsely claiming that the footage came straight from the raging war. *The Heathen Chinese and the Sunday School Teacher* (AM&B, 1904), a five-scene melodrama, portrayed Sunday school teachers who are lured into an opium den and smoking dope, until police arrive and arrest the Chinese drug pushers.

Overseas, the growing popularity of motion pictures mirrored the developments in the United States. In Russia, the Coronation of Nicholas II was captured in a newsreel (1896), but an event two days later in which the Tsar was to introduce his wife to the citizens erupted into a riot, and the scenes of countless men and women being trampled to death were seized from the cameramen by soldiers trying to restore calm. Despite the fact that motion pictures were only invented a few years prior to the coronation, the political power of the event was apparent even to the Tsar's police.

In England, the political power of the medium was evident in the production *The Bengal Lancers in Peking* (1901), which was produced during the Boxer Rebellion. At the same time, in South

FIGURE 3.6. Sound newsreel interview with Thomas Edison. 1926. Footagesource.com

Africa, the Boer War was captured by Thomas Edison in a staged newsreel titled *Boers Bringing In British Prisoners* (1900). Another newsreel features a staged battle in which the British emerge victorious, *English Lancers Charging* (1900).

1920s

By the mid-1920s, all major studios began to offer newsreel services to augment their feature-film shows. Most studios began producing a newsreel program delivered on Mondays and Thursdays, giving audiences a relatively recent look at events around the world. They soon added sound and featured politics, fashion, natural disasters and most other stories ripped from the headlines of newspapers.

1930s TO 1960s

Some call this the Golden Age of newsreels. Several newsreel companies continued producing two newsreel presentations, shown

FIGURE 3.7. Newsreel coverage of eruption of Mt. St Helens. May 18, 1980. Footagesource.com

weekly in thousands of theaters across the United States and Europe. Despite competition from television news stories, international news on a large screen continued to thrill audiences and newsreels would continue to be part of the movie-going experience for more than three decades.

Many of these newsreels still exist today in several archives, both in the United States and in various countries in Europe.

1950s TO THE PRESENT

In the early 1950s, television stations began to offer news programs along with their entertainment shows. During this period no videotape existed, so they had to shoot their news stories on film and "roll them in" to the evening news broadcast. This technology stayed in existence until the first video news cameras became popular in the early 1980s.

Newsreel services understood the worth of archival material and footage deemed historic was vaulted. Film has proven itself to be a stable medium. Videotape is another story. The problem is that video emulsion is much less stable than film, and tapes from the latter part of the twentieth century are beginning to shed their emulsion base and thus their ability to be replayed and copied.

21ST CENTURY

From the early 2000s to the present, digital cameras have defined newsreel capture and playback. The hi-definition quality is a definite plus. The number of news services together with an army of citizen journalists have allowed for almost a twenty-four–hour news cycle to be immediately available to viewers.

The one negative is the difficulty archiving this quantity of material. Many news services erase their tapes when finished downloading their material. Citizen journalists may keep their material on hard drives that have fairly short lives before they crash. The age of digital has proven itself to be a mixed blessing for archivists.

✿ SUMMARY

The newsreel goes back to the earliest days of motion pictures. Hundreds of thousands of newsreels were produced on film from the turn of the last century to the late 1970s. Television stations moved to videotape during this time and have captured daily events ever since.

Several libraries contain substantial newsreel archives. This material is available for licensing (see Part Three) and is substantially less expensive compared to major studio feature films.

CHAPTER 4

HOME MOVIES

- **Type of medium:** 1920 to 1940s, 16mm.
- 1940s to 1970s, 8mm.
- Late 1970s to early 2000, tape.
- Early 2000 to present, digital.
- **Years in use:** 1920s to the present.
- **Copyright status:** Gray. See chapter 24.

FIGURE 4.1. Disneyland, 1956. Home movie. Footagesource.com

✿ INTRODUCTION

Making films was never an inexpensive effort. Cost of raw stock, developing the film and the investment in a camera made the entry tough for the first three decades of filmmaking. However, by the 1920s, the less expensive 16mm format found popularity among affluent homes and businesses that wanted to take part in the motion picture revolution. For the next three decades, thousands of home movies were shot that captured life at home and work.

✿ GOLDEN AGE OF HOME MOVIES: THE 8MM FILM

Beginning in the late 1930s, a less expensive 8mm camera and projector became popular, opening filmmaking to middle-class families. For the next four decades, 8mm (and later Super 8mm) became the standard for capturing Christmas, birthdays and special events around the world. During the early 1960s, color processing costs had come down. Hundreds of thousands of these films survive and are readily found in family closets and at thrift shops around the world.

FIGURE 4.2. Christmas celebration. Home movie from the 1950s. Footagesource.com

∽ SPOTLIGHT ON . . .

Filmmaker STUART A. GOLDMAN, producer of *Elvis Home Movies*

Archival footage can make a documentary come alive and seem more credible, especially if the material directly supports the story in some way. Producing my most recent Elvis film, Elvis Home Movies, *I incorporated what is believed to be the oldest film footage of Elvis Presley in a private setting, taken during a vacation in Biloxi, Mississippi, July, 1956.*

The interview subjects in the film talk about the relationship of Elvis and his mother. In the home movie footage, which has been used in a number of Elvis documentaries, we see Gladys actually feeding Elvis a peanut butter-and-banana sandwich while he's busy fishing! She was known to be a very caring (if not over-protective)

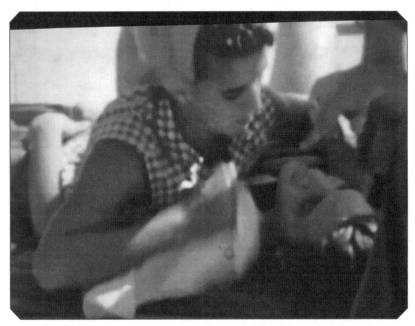

FIGURE 4.3. *Elvis Home Movies.* Photo courtesy of Stuart Goldman.

parent and the footage clearly shows it! The film clip strengthens the story line immensely.

In addition, Elvis's girlfriend at this time, June Juanico, can be seen in the footage lying on the deck of the rented boat with Elvis, kissing and hugging affectionately. Viewers might not believe this happened if someone just said so in the film. But the footage illustrates what their relationship was really like.

STUART A. GOLDMAN
Producer

❧ VIDEOTAPE CAMCORDER

When the home video recorder was introduced in the early 1970s, they were expensive and utilized the somewhat unwieldy 1" reel-to-reel videotape. Eight millimeter film cassettes were easier to use and the world did not adopt home video recording.

A decade later, the introduction of VHS videocassettes proved to have an entirely different reception. Easy to use and affordable to buy, it was only natural that families should be able to shoot their home movies and play them at home. The video camcorder became an immediate hit, and millions of home movies were shot in VHS and similar formats over the next two decades.

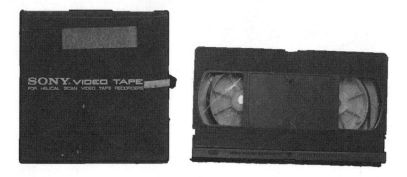

FIGURE 4.4. VHS and 1" reel-to-reel and VHS video formats from the 1970s and 1980s. Footagesource.com

One can often find these tapes at rummage sales for little if any cost. They are a great source of establishing footage for the 1980s and 1990s, but they have two limitations. The first is that filmmakers should generally have a clearance for any people appearing in the image. The second is that the first generation of VHS tapes do not have a shelf life beyond ten years. After that, the emulsion base begins flaking and the tapes eventually have no image left on them.

DIGITAL AGE OF HOME MOVIES

By the early 2000s, digital, hi-definition consumer cameras that hooked up to televisions were available for a few hundred dollars. When smartphones became popular, built-in cameras offered nearly equal quality.

FIGURE 4.5. Hi-def home movie capturing Kim Kardashian shopping in Beverly Hills. Footagesource.com

In the space of four decades, home movies moved from 8mm film, analog tape, digital tape and finally to today's hard-drive-based-memory video recording.

Home Video Format Overview

ANALOG

- 16mm
- 8mm
- Analog Tape Formats
  - 1"
  - VHS and VHS/C
  - BETA
  - HI 8

DIGITAL

- Mini DV (*digital video*)
- SD cards, consumer camera and smartphones

SUMMARY

Home movies are an affordable source of footage representing the past century. They were shot by millions of people and many films and tapes still survive. They are a great source of establishing time periods, fashions, locations and lifestyles.

There are some limitations to re-using the material you may uncover. Be aware that they do not adhere to the same copyright protection that commercial films do. These films were typically never originally copyrighted and thus can always be copyrighted as new works. I personally learned this back in 1980 when working on my first television show for KNBC in Los Angeles. We were doing a half-hour show about a famous local clergyman who was cele-brating his eightieth birthday. His secretary asked if we would be interested in including a home movie from a wedding he officiated at in 1930. We gratefully accepted the offer and the show aired with this footage the following Sunday morning.The next day the show's producer got a call from the daughter of the couple in the wedding home movie. She was very angry, claiming the film was produced by professionals and owned by the family and she threatened to sue. The producer came to me and asked if I had gotten their permission. I didn't even know they existed and told her that the secretary had given it to us. I came very close to ending my film career then and there.

You cannot be careful enough. By being hyper-focused about the possible issues and solving them beforehand, you save yourself a lot of potential grief when your show gets seen by an audience.

CHAPTER 5

BROADCAST TELEVISION

- **Type of medium:** Analog and digital video.
- **Years:** 1926 to the present.
- **Audience:** Worldwide.
- **Copyright status:** Mix of public domain and copyright. See chapter 24.

INTRODUCTION

Millions of hours of television programming exists, coming from nearly every region of the world and spanning over eighty years of production. Television programming is tied to a series of

FIGURE 5.1. Behind the scenes of a TV production. *Tomorrow Television*. 1946. Footagesource.com

important technological factors that have determined its look, feel and reach.

Beginning about eight decades ago, video transmission has become the predominant entertainment medium throughout the world and offers the largest amount of archival media material available.

✒ HOW TELEVISION CAME ABOUT

From the late 1890s to the late 1920s a group of scientists from around the world worked on creating a transmission system that would capture an image and send it electronically to another location. The technology of a working television was claimed by two competing American scientists in the late 1920s, Philo Farnsworth and RCA-backed Vladimir Zworkin. While the inventors of television fought it out in court, others used their technology to test it and see how they could profit.

Within a few years, experimental television stations were operating around the country, including one owned by Paramount Studios in Hollywood, California. The images were archaic compared to today but allowed for the rollout of a working television system nationwide.

It turned out that the 1930s was a difficult period to bring out a new and expensive technology. The Depression hurt all entertainment, including cutting audience attendance in half at movie theaters. Few people had extra income to buy into an experimental entertainment device and those that did bought the relatively affordable radio.

RCA and others continued to improve the television, and with public fanfare, RCA showed off its video camera at the 1939 World's Fair. The rollout of television however would once again be delayed for almost a full decade due to the outbreak of World War II.

FIGURE 5.2. Watching early TV show, circa 1950. Footagesource.com

1950s TO THE EARLY 2000s

After World War II, television stations began to open in most major cities across the United States. Radio networks NBC and CBS expanded their media operations to include television, beginning the first domestic television network systems.

Video programs that were produced during these early days in studios do not exist anymore except for a rare few that were recorded by a "kinescope" process, a film camera typically shooting a monitor of the program while in progress.

Other shows during this time were actually produced on film and sent to TV stations. Legend has it that the original Desi and Lucy show was broadcast live as a half-hour comedy, but Lucy and Desi wanted to keep copies for themselves and had each episode filmed too. This was the birth of syndicated shows.

FIGURE 5.3. Lucy and Desi public service announcement. Footagesource.com

ERA OF VIDEOTAPE

Television programming would not have succeeded if it weren't for the development of videotape. Network programmers wanted a system in which they could produce a show live on the east coast and replay it three hours later in the west coast, something impossible until 1956. That year Ampex Corporation released their 2" quad videotape. This allowed programmers to produce a show and then replay it when it fit their schedule.

After two decades of storing tape on the bulky 2" tapes, a better quality 1" tape was introduced in 1975. Over the next two decades, all shows mastered for airing were put on 1" tape and 2" disappeared.

As family life moved to the suburbs, television promised viewers a new way to entertain kids in the morning and the adults at night.

Companies such as RCA owned both the TV networks as well as production of television sets, and they cross-promoted buying and watching television. Famous radio shows suddenly were turned into TV shows and film actors like Milton Berle moved to the small tube. By 1960 there were over 50 million sets in the United States; a set in nine out of ten homes. Television had solidly become a part of everyday life around the world.

Most of this material was shot on a boxlike 4:3 format. While original material could be over 700 lines of resolution when shot with Beta SP cameras in the 1990s, most home televisions could not exceed 500 lines of resolution.

FIGURE 5.4. 2" quad video tape (in the rear), 1" tape and Betacam SP. Footagesource.com

During the early 1970s, Sony introduced a format for corporate and educational use, ¾" U-matic. This cassette was ideal for recording and editing programs for non-broadcast use, and was widely put in use for nearly a quarter of a century. Archives today still have thousands of these tapes and hundreds of thousands of hours of original programs remain on them.

In 1986 Sony perfected its Betacam, creating a Superior Performance (Beta SP) tape. The quality was nearly as good as 1" plus its cassettes were small and could be used for shooting news, field stories and mastering tapes for broadcast. It soon became the workhorse for almost every TV station news division in the country and was not replaced until digital media came in during the late 1990s.

NETWORKS AND LOCAL STATIONS PROGRAMMING

Television in the United States had several different ownership levels.

CBS, ABC, NBC, and Dumont represented the original television networks. They supplied evening programming and network news. Each of these networks was allowed to own seven stations, referred to as O and O (owned and operated), usually located in the large cities like Los Angeles and New York.

The second strata were affiliate stations. These were owned by separate companies but aired the network programming that they were affiliated with.

The final group was independent stations. They did not have network affiliation and aired programming purchased through distributors. Examples of this include *Judge Judy* first run programs and *Seinfeld* re-runs.

Key Terms:

1. Network. A media network is composed of a combination of media outlets around the country, together with the production of content for their stations and affiliated stations.

2. First-Run Syndication. TV programs that are aimed at non-network television. Shows like *Judge Judy* are available to all markets, and the highest bidding station gets the show.

3. Studio. The studio system, created at the turn of the twentieth century, combined under one corporate structure the development, production and distribution of films and, later, television shows. Studios today are different from their earlier versions in that most are subsidiaries of much larger media organizations that wanted the large libraries of films and television shows that the studios held.

4. Independents. Producers not affiliated with large studios are known as "independents." This includes legendary producers like Roger Corman who produced several films a year but avoided being told by major studios what to produce.

5. Local Stations. Local stations refer to TV stations located in a city. They may be an independent station, an affiliate of a network or a station actually owned by a network.

6. Television Programs. Live early shows, shot on film off the monitor kinescope, 1926 to the early 1960s. In the early 1960s Ampex introduced videotape and programs could be recorded and archived on 2" tape. This was replaced in the 1970s by 1" reel-to-reel.

7. Commercials. Most commercials were shot and sent out as 16mm film elements. In the late 1970s, advertisers began delivering their advertising on videotape to stations.

8. News Programs. News was part of every TV station's programming. Most shows have not survived the years but some stations have kept kinescopes and tape of important broadcasts.

9. News Packages. Station reporters shot millions of feet of 16mm film recording daily events. In the late 1970s cameras changed

to video format, staying analog with the standard Beta SP recorders until digital media replaced these in the early 2000s.

10. **Public Affairs.** All stations were mandated by the Federal Communications Commission rules to offer programming that would benefit the community at large and public affairs programming became part of all station programming up to the 1980s when these rules were relaxed. Many of these shows were originally shot on film or kinescope and survive, a testimony of the various societal battles that have occurred over the decades.

11. **Cartoons.** Weekend morning cartoons were produced by studios for local stations. Most were delivered on film up to the 1970s and later on tape formats.

SHIFT FROM ANALOG TO DIGITAL

The most pronounced change in broadcast television began to occur around 2000. Up to this point, programming was shot in a 4:3 format and analog signals usually contained 500 lines of resolution or less. Within the next decade, the majority of the world's millions of analog televisions went to the landfill as digital media allowed for hi-definition widescreen televisions delivering over 1,000 lines of resolution.

On the professional front, hi-definition cameras and video editing systems were perfected and allowed post-production technology to offer an increase in the visual quality of shows at a price unheard of just a few years back.

What does this mean for you and your quest for the best image quality? First, most material created after the early 2000s is in hi-definition. Second, most material created between 1893 and the early 2000s is substantially inferior in picture quality. One can enhance old images, but as the old saying goes, you cannot get blood out of a turnip. I have worked with producers over the past few years who have forgotten this lesson and have gotten upset when a 1950 newsreel is not hi-definition nor widescreen. You will have to patiently remind your clients that each generation offered the best it could and that it is too bad that hi-definition was not invented in 1920, but it wasn't!

☙ SUMMARY

The good news is that archival video material is readily available. Hundreds of millions of clips exist online that represent video content spanning nearly eighty years.

The bad news is that just because it is on a file-sharing site does not mean that the copyright owner is giving you permission to re-use their material.

The other limiting factor is quality of image. Most video available on file-sharing has been compressed many times and is a fraction of the quality of its original. Unless you can find a site that allows you to download an uncompressed version of the original, you are getting a video that will not reproduce well.

CHAPTER 6

CABLE TV

- **Type of medium:** Programming sent over cable via satellite transmission.
- **Years in use:** Early 1960s to the present.
- **Audience:** Global, usually in urban areas.
- **Copyright status:** Copyrighted material.

❦ INTRODUCTION

Cable TV began as a simple "retransmission" technology, where homes that could not be reached by tower signals could be better served by a wired hookup.

FIGURE 6.1. Satellite receiving dishes. Courtesy NASA.

With satellite technology beginning in the mid 1960s, cable entrepreneurs began to envision sending signals from different regions to these cable hookups and entice more people to subscribe. The first major commercial success was the introduction of Ted Turner's Atlanta station WTCG in 1976. The idea of retransmission was copied by other stations, including Illinois station WGN, and getting hooked up to cable meant more than just getting better local reception. You could watch used car vendors from Chicago as well as the weather report from Atlanta. It was exciting times.

By the early 1980s Turner and other cable pioneers began to add new stations to the roster of satellite-supplied programming. CNN, *the* 24-hour-news channel, was the big game changer, going on the air in June, 1980. By the mid-1980s millions of Americans were watching programming with niche audience identification—such as CNN (news), Discovery (documentaries), and Lifetime (women's interests)—and the era of TV network domination began to erode.

Today, with approximately forty domestic cable networks operating, the amount of programming is astounding. The type of material available that has been produced for cable networks includes:

- Nature documentaries
- War documentaries
- Hollywood history documentaries
- Made-for-cable feature films
- Cartoons
- News
- Cooking shows

Top domestic cable networks:

Premium
- HBO
- Starz Encore
- Showtime

Basic

- Discovery
- A&E (Arts and Entertainment)
- ESPN

Top three cable TV companies:

- Comcast
- AT&T
- Time Warner

Many cable networks do not produce their own programming, but license it. The best place to start figuring out who owns the rights to a show that you might like to acquire footage from is to go to the IMDbPro website and contact the production company.

FIGURE 6.2. *Hollywood Dinosaur Chronicles.* Discovery Channel. Documentaries on the Discovery Channel started out being focused on science, nature and war and oriented toward men. Discovery Communications has grown to include several niche audience channels since it first went on the air in the 1980s. Forsher Productions.

SUMMARY

With dozens of channels and hundreds of programs, cable programming offers an incredible amount of material to help you research and find footage appropriate to your project.

The limitations with cable programming have to do with clearing rights. Programming that appears on cable channels constitutes a true hodgepodge of ownership headaches. Any show might have several of the following owners that would have to be cleared if you wanted to re-use their program's content:

- Original producer
- Program's foreign or domestic distributor
- The Cable Channel

On top of this, many of these shows are non-fiction programs composed of archival footage. While you may have access to the show, the footage you want may have come from a third-party source.

My experience is that these programs are a great source for research but should not be the primary source for acquiring archival footage.

CHAPTER 7

HOME VIDEO

- **Type of medium:** Programming delivered through videotape cassettes and streaming.
- **Years in use:** Early 1960s to the present.
- **Audience:** Global.
- **Copyright status:** Public domain and copyrighted material.

❦ INTRODUCTION

The broadcast and cable world would soon have some serious competition. In 1975, Sony introduced its consumer-based videotape recorder, the Betamax. The new technology was expensive and very little product was available to play on the machine. Rival JVC soon came out with their VHS format and licensed this to other manufacturers, causing the VHS format to be popularly adopted.

FIGURE 7.1.
1982. Sony
Betamax recorder.
Footagesource.com

❧ HOME VIDEOCASSETTE PERIOD

During the earliest years of home video players, very little home entertainment was available. Studios saw the VCR as copyright infringement devices and sued Sony. In the 1984 Sony Betamax Decision, the US Supreme Court ruled that the VCRs were for home use only and did not break US copyright laws. Up to 1984, few studios wanted to release their titles and video players and recorder machines were limited to playing either home video recordings or public domain movies. After 1984, the floodgates opened and thousands of titles were released to a built-up audience of millions who had bought these machines.

WHAT YOU WILL FIND

There are three very different types of content in home video programming. The first are classic films and television shows. These are from the studio archives and typically are owned by those studios.

The second type of programming is "made for home video" releases. Starting in the early 1980s, thousands of these were produced and targeted to niche audiences. You will find a multitude of "how to" videos, travel videos, documentaries, vanity pieces and pretty much anything that a mainstream studio or distributor didn't want to bother with.

Finally, thousands of "classic" titles not released by major studios exist. In the early days of home video, these were entirely public domain films and television shows. Despite the audience for DVD titles shrinking, copyrighted titles continue to be released, with producers believing that making even a few thousand dollars a year was better than nothing.

The world of home video has a lot to offer you. You can get your hands on titles relatively easily. Many titles are not owned by studios and you can often negotiate affordable license agreements.

However, like everything in the entertainment industry, you need to carry out your due diligence. The first step is to locate and screen the title. The second is to find out who the legal owner is.

⌒ *SPOTLIGHT ON . . .*

THE BIRTH OF HOME VIDEO

Spectacular Disasters

George Takei's Spectacular Disasters *is a home video release I produced in 1987. The concept was simple: George Takei hosted and narrated a show that explored how newsreel cameramen captured the greatest catastrophes of the first six decades of the twentieth century. It examined both natural and man-made disasters.*

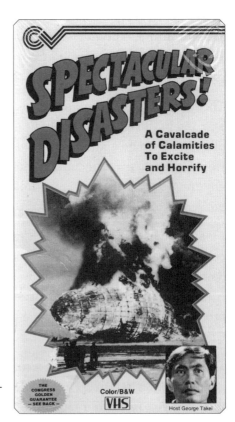

FIGURE 7.2. *Spectacular Disasters.* 1987. Early "sell-through" home video title. Thousands of original productions were produced specifically for the home-video market during the 1980s and 1990s. Forsher Productions.

This show was produced at a time when nobody knew what to expect from home video. We decided to try and make a title that would appeal to a wide audience and spend as little as money on it as possible. This meant one day in the studio with George and a week editing the show.

My two fellow producers thought it would do well due to its subject matter. The German word schadenfreude *means "taking pleasure in other people's discomfort," and as producers, we knew that many films and television shows had this as their core ingredient.*

The show was offered as a "sell-through." This means it was not meant for rentals but sold at a price point that attracted impulse buyers. In its first six months, our distributor reported well in excess of ten thousand sales. At ten dollars a cassette, the distributors were very happy.

✿ THE DVD TAKES OVER

In the early 1990s, nearly two decades after the earliest videocassettes began shaping the home media market, Phillip, Sony and Toshiba agreed on a disc format, which became known as the DVD. The new technology had a number of improvements over VHS tape. The first was that it wasn't tape and subject to wear-and-tear issues that plagued VHS cassettes. The DVD was also searchable, allowing audiences to go to different parts of the story or to additional content in a click or two.

By 2003, increases in demand for hi-definition content allowed for the introduction of the Blu-ray disc, similar to the DVD but allowing a substantially greater amount of video content on each disc. It proved popular but, due to technological advances, would not be the last word in home video delivery.

The original home video revolution lasted nearly two decades. Blockbuster Video stores could be found on every corner and filmmakers in Hollywood found a convenient way to finance their films by selling home video rights for considerable amounts. Unfortunately, nothing lasts forever, and despite the increased quality of DVD and Blu-ray recordings offered, video streaming cut sales dramatically. By the early 2000s, home video as a primary funding source for films began to erode.

What can you find in the world of home video? In addition to access to thousands of major studio releases, thousands of producers produced programming specifically targeted to home video use. Copies of these films are readily available on Amazon, eBay and other online sources. These are a fantastic source of accessing viewing copies of material you might need without dealing with studios or archives.

The tricky part to using "made for home video" titles is locating the copyright holder for licensing. Many home video titles were produced by small production companies and released by independent distributors. The majority of both production companies and distributors creating this product have long since closed. The smartest of these producers have taken their original materials and licensed them for representation by one of the major independent film archives. (More about this in Part Three.)

The major studios are typically (but not always) the copyright holders of feature-film titles they release and you can contact the studio's legal affairs department to license material you found on home videocassettes or DVDs.

☙ HI-DEFINITION AND STREAMING

The most pronounced change since 2000 is how we watch home video programming. In 2000, video was shot and offered on a 4:3 format and the analog-capture technology offered at best 550 lines of resolution. Within a decade, all of the "state of the art" analog televisions went to the landfill as digital media allowed for 16:9

7.3a. The interview was shot in 1983 on 16mm film and converted to SD analog video.

7.3b. Thirty years later, it was transferred again to hi-definition video, enhancing the image quality by nearly double. Footagesource.com

FIGURES 7.3a and 7.3b. Interview with producer Hal Roach, creator of Laurel and Hardy and the Little Rascals.

format hi-definition widescreen televisions delivering over 1,000 lines of resolution. The next few years promise an expansion to even higher levels of resolution.

Editing systems were perfected and allowed post-production technology that increased the quality of shows at a price unheard of just a few years back.

SUMMARY

What does this mean for you and your quest for good quality video? Once again, most material created after the early 2000s is in hi-definition. Second, most material created between 1893 and the early 2000s is substantially inferior in picture quality.

PROGRAMMING COMMONLY FOUND ON HOME VIDEOCASSETTES.

- Features
- TV shows
- Animation
- Documentaries
- Exercise shows

CHAPTER 8

INTERNET

- **Type of medium:** Internet-based entertainment.
- **Years in use:** Early 2000s to the present.
- **Audience:** Global.
- **Copyright status:** Copyrighted.

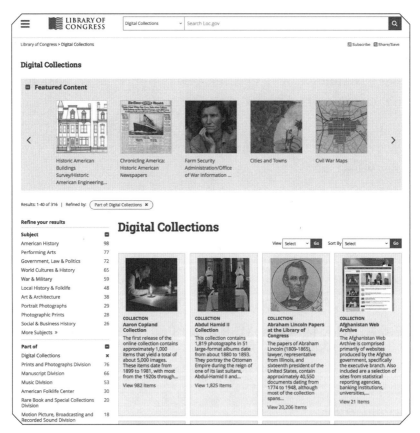

FIGURE 8.1. Library of Congress portal. One click and you are on your way to accessing hundreds of thousands of films and photos. Library of Congress.

❧ INTRODUCTION

Up to the year 2000, video entertainment had seen three major technologies make its products commercially available: broadcast television, cable television and pre-recorded home video product. Beginning in the early 2000s, advances in computer processer speed along with improvements in compression of digital video signals made streaming of video commercially viable.

Everyone saw the potential of internet-based entertainment coming as early as the mid 1990s, but it took over a decade before it began to become commercially mainstream. In 2000, if you wanted to send a 30-second video to a friend over AOL, you could expect download times of two or three minutes. YouTube began beta-testing in 2005, and by July, 2006, over 65,000 new videos were being uploaded daily. It was the dawn of the age of internet streaming.

YouTube and other video-sharing sites have dramatically challenged all the old rules of copyright and public domain. Studios began to see many of their films posted to file-sharing sites. Some studios were happy, believing that these clips promoted their classic titles. Other studios sued, the most famous being Viacom vs. YouTube in 2007. This case was in the courts for nearly seven years, with both parties settling in the end with the agreement that basically said YouTube would pull film clips if a copyright owner requested it.

❧ STREAMING VIDEO SITES ARE THE NEW CABLE CHANNELS

Billions of dollars of programming have shifted from conventional cable channels to streaming sites like Netflix and Amazon. Some of the best shows are now available on your smartphone.

The good news is that tens of thousands of hours of relatively recently produced archival video material is readily available. Ease of access, however, doesn't mean it's free to re-use. Just because it is on a file-sharing site does not mean that the copyright owner is giving you permission to re-use their material.

The other limiting factor is quality of image. Most video available on file-sharing sites has been compressed many times and is a fraction of the quality of its original. Unless you can find a site that allows you to download an uncompressed version of the original, you are getting a video that will not reproduce well.

WHAT IS AVAILABLE

Almost everything—for a price. That is both a great step forward for archival researchers and a curse for producers. Archives typically stream their available footage directly to you for research. Studio material is also available through streaming. Public domain material is flooding the file-sharing sites.

WEBISODES

An army of producers has created thousands of short-form shows commonly referred to as webisodes. They can range from talk shows shot in a garage to expensive dramatic stories shot with expensive equipment on location.

What makes webisodes interesting are the multitude of shows that have been produced—most requiring their producers to self-fund their projects. A successful webisode on a YouTube channel must get more than 20,000 subscribers before the advertising income begins to generate a very modest part-time income. With thousands of channels competing for eyeballs, this is no easy task. However, the thousands of shows online today offer a tremendous amount of contemporary archival material at affordable prices. Most producers of these programs are very receptive to affordable license agreements.

BLOGS

Blogs are online diaries. They can be simple updates about life or feature video (referred to as *vlogs*), music, artwork and other media elements.

Millions of these exist. One can locate them by a search for specific themes. These also provide researchers with a potential treasure trove of usable material for an affordable price.

IMAGES

Dozens of sites are dedicated to sharing images and ideas. Instagram, Google, Facebook, Bing and Twitter have created huge followings worldwide.

You can use these sites for researching current interests and trends. You can also find images that might work for your projects.

Internet-based productions commonly focus on the following themes:

- Movie reviews
- Politics
- Personal philosophy
- Music
- Sci Fi
- Young adult programming
- Educational "how tos"

⌐ *SPOTLIGHT ON . . .*

CHRIS ALLEN, Blogger

I've been making podcasts for about three years now. I don't directly use any archival material on the show, there's no images or video, or even old audio recordings. A lot of my research comes from old newspapers, which I'm really happy are all online now. Through public

FIGURE 8.2. Chris Allen, "The Seattle Files" blog. Courtesy of Chris Allen.

library websites I can access any American newspaper between the late 1700s up to today. They are scanned as PDF files and, even better, are searchable. It makes things a lot easier than having to go through microfilm.

I always spend a lot more time researching the episodes than recording them. On the show I teach stories about local history to local comedians, they riff on it, so it is both comedy and education, so I want to make sure I know as much about the story as I possibly can. It's usually around ten hours of research for one hour of recording, then about an hour of post-production, typically just editing out long pauses or breaths, or if someone said something inappropriate. (The show has swearing and no rating, but sometimes someone says something I think makes them look bad and I want them to look good, so I'll cut it out.)

I haven't had any sponsors on the show, although I have been contacted by some people who wanted to have me include ads for their businesses. I always turned them down since my listenership wasn't large enough to warrant asking for enough money to make it worth my while. I also was hesitant to give up any creative control or receive input on the content of the show.

There are certain businesses, like Audible, where you don't have to strike a deal with them for sponsorship, you just create an account with them and they create a special URL such as audible.com/mypodcast, which you then plug on the show, and if people go to that specific URL and buy their services you get a cut.

I had a fair amount of success with Patreon, which is a crowd-funding site, but instead of trying to get one large amount to fund a project like you do with Kickstarter or Indiegogo, people set up to make ongoing contributions. It really only works once you've already built an audience, then say, hey, I make this thing and give it away for free, if you want me to keep making it, kick me one or two dollars a month. By the end of my run I was getting a few hundred dollars a month in small contributions.

There was also the option of charging per episode, but the large pod catchers like iTunes and Stitcher won't let you charge, so it would be difficult for the audience to find it.

I have close to 200,000 downloads as of writing this, and even though I haven't made a new episode in months I still have about 200 downloads a day now, so the number of listeners is still growing. I've done some targeted social media ad buys which have worked reasonably well. The show that I made was specific to one area, so if I was doing an episode about a specific neighborhood, I could do an ad buy for just one square mile, and target people in that area that "like" other things that are similar to what I make.

The best, by far, method of building an audience has been word of mouth. I know people who do everything "right," they have their branding down, their marketing game is on point, but they never manage to build an audience. The majority of people who listen to my podcast are people who had friends recommend it to them. I think the show makes people feel smart, they are able to say at a party or walking down the street, hey, I learned this thing recently, it's pretty interesting, you should check it out. Most people I know who make podcasts of web series or anything online spend more time on their promotion then they do on their product. People like to make things that you can "share" on social media, but when you share something that is making a statement that you want people to associate you with, that thing you are sharing, is the thing you are making something people will want to associate themselves with?

Along those lines, creating fun and interesting headlines that draw people in and get them to click in the first place is helpful. Have the first statement be a question, or starting the sentence with the word "you" are good ways to draw people in immediately. The other is wording things to be as tantalizing as possible. I did an episode on serial killer Billy Gohl, but if I just named the episode "Billy Gohl" no one would know who that is, so instead I called it "The Ghoul of Greys Harbor," which was one of his nicknames. Same with an episode on Woodland Park Zoo, which I called "War on Monkey Island," which was a small aspect of the story, but a more interesting title. The most downloaded episode by far is "The Holy Rollers Sex Cult," for obvious reasons.

CHRIS ALLEN
The Seattle Files

❧ SUMMARY

The internet allows you to both research and find archival material for your projects. It has made searching for material considerably easier than it was just a decade ago.

The internet has grown in just a decade from a technology best used to send a simple email to the primary mechanism to distribute video content in the world. Almost every idea that anyone wants to spend time and energy putting together has been produced as a webisode, blog or vlog. Hundreds of thousands of blogs and vlogs exist and YouTube and Vimeo hold literally millions of programs.

The number one rule is that if you find material that you want for your project, you will need to get a full clearance from the creator. This will require you to find out who the legal owner is and where to contact them. (See Part Three, chapter 24, "Understanding the Law 101.")

CHAPTER 9

COMMERCIALS

- **Type of medium:** Film, video and streaming.
- **Years in use:** 1890s to the present.
- **Audience:** Global.
- **Copyright status:** Both public domain and copyright. Trademark issues also involved.

FIGURE 9.1. 1950s television shows were often sponsored by major corporations. Footagesource.com

❦ INTRODUCTION

Commercial advertisements began in the United States with the publication of Benjamin Franklin's *Pennsylvania Gazette* in 1729. By the middle of the nineteenth century, over 5,000 newspapers were in publication and advertisements made up a substantial income base for their publishers. It was a perfect match. As soon as newspaper audiences began purchasing papers in large numbers, retailers realized they had a captive audience for pitching their product. From this simple beginning, commercials have developed to be the economic engine—either directly or indirectly—driving most of our mass media over the past century. Early commercial advertisements are also a fantastic source of archival material, featuring famous performers and visuals representing how we lived over the past century.

FIGURE 9.2. Advertisement from 1880s newspaper. Footagesource.com

🐾 1880s: BRAND PRINT ADVERTISING

With the multitude of newspapers and magazines being printed, advertisers took advantage of having artists create an image that would become a "brand" to their product. The most famous brands today include the Apple logo, the Nike Swoosh and the name Coca-Cola.

Print media soon began to present dozens of advertisements that tied together a written description of the product with the "brand" design.

🐾 EARLY CINEMA HOUSE COMMERCIALS

The first projected films started in the early 1900s and as soon as audiences sat in the theater, nickel theater owners figured out that they could get some extra money by showing simple advertisements from slides between films.

🐾 1920s–1950s

By 1922, the United States had over 4,000 movie theaters. Slides with advertising were still shown in theaters, but advertisers and studios decided that they could produce short films that told stories, forerunners of today's commercials and infomercials. These included the likes of legendary actress Bette Davis telling her kids that they aren't getting a bike but a defense bond instead, a public service announcement (PSA) for the War Department that was shown before the feature film in theaters during World War II.

Radio programming also became popular at this time, and all programming was "sponsored." That meant audio commercials soon became common and musical jingles, famous actor spokespersons and dramatic scripts all competed for the audience's attention. Thousands of hours of programming from this period still survive.

FIGURE 9.3. Bette Davis appears in a World War II public service announcement, circa 1943, promoting the purchase of Defense Bonds. Footagesource.com

Finally, newspapers and magazines added color printing technology and advertising inserts. Advertising agencies adopted "cross promotion" during this period, using stars to promote items in print, radio and even short programs at the theater. Studios also developed "coming attraction" trailers that promoted upcoming films. Many of these early trailers were never separately copyrighted and serve as a great source of showing Hollywood productions without using copyrighted films.

✿ PUBLIC SERVICE ANNOUNCEMENTS

This was also the period in which the public service announcement was introduced. Often produced by a government or non-profit agency (and thus often public domain), PSAs featured big stars and timely events. They are a tremendous source of period footage, often with famous stars, at an affordable price.

FIGURE 9.4. Comedian Phyllis Diller appears in a 1960s Savings Bond public service announcement hour special. Footagesource.com

🐚 1950s–2000: AGE OF TELEVISION ADVERTISEMENT

The major addition to the commercial offerings available to the public began around 1950 when television sets became more popular around the country. Advertisers, using the same model they used for radio advertising (and often the same spokespeople), began to reach out to TV audiences. These commercials were either standalone or actually built into a TV show. Milton Berle and Jack Benny would tell a joke and then seamlessly change the subject to their favorite car, cigarette or milk product.

Theaters were losing audiences to TV and realized they had to find new ways of making money. Feeding audiences popcorn became very popular and theaters began to create self-promotion advertisements for their concessions. One can find wonderful ads touting

FIGURE 9.5. Buick TV commercial from the 1950s. Footagesource.com

popcorn, soft drinks and special holiday offerings throughout this period.

Advertisers also decided that a movie audience would respond to commercials put on large theater screens, modeled after regular TV commercials but larger, louder and longer. Over the past three decades, special commercials produced for theaters have become part of the movie-going experience.

In the early 1980s, home video entertainment surpassed theatrical screening in income produced and advertisers tried to take advantage of this new way to reach audiences. Trailers from studios could soon be found on home videocassettes and DVDs, and advertisers began to put their product within the film or TV show. Thus actors began drinking name beverages, eating name cereals and walking past name stores.

2000–PRESENT

The big change in advertising is the combination of the internet, computer databases and search engines. We are now living in a world in which your personal interests are sent via your smartphone and computer to databases at search engines that sell this information to sponsors. This gives advertisers the ability to target their product to people who are looking for it. The world of commercials has gone from giant "shout outs" where advertisers were hoping a few people would listen to targeted advertising where ads are sent to only the most likely customers.

For those looking for archival product representing different times over the past century, advertising is an affordable and often times well-produced source of material. Many advertisements were never copyrighted. Advertisers are often happy to have their brand shown, even if it is from a nostalgic perspective.

If you want images from an advertiser, you might even be able to offer a barter by which your show ties to the advertiser's product. In exchange for the advertisers getting visuals they own, you get to have material shown for free. Strange new world.

❦ WHAT MATERIAL IS AVAILABLE IN COMMERCIALS?

- Music
- Radio programs
- Internet
- Cinematic commercials
- Film trailers
- Clothing
- Drugs

- Cross promotions
- Women
- Children
- Teen

SUMMARY

Print, film and television advertising serve as a great source of material for your projects. It includes material dating back nearly three centuries and up to last week. Commercials portray different times in our history: fashions, pop culture icons, foods, architecture and almost every aspect of life both in the United States and abroad. Many advertisements were never copyrighted or the copyrights have expired.

Advertisers still need to be treated with some concern, since large companies have trademarks on their logos and protect them very carefully. Famous actors also must be cleared separately since they can claim to be a brand unto themselves. See Part Two for finding commercials and Part Three for clearing the material.

CHAPTER 10

ANIMATION

- **Type of medium:** Film, digital.
- **Years in use:** Late 1890s to the present.
- **Audience:** Worldwide.
- **Copyright status:** Pre-early 1920s, public domain. 1920s to 1970s, mixture of pubic domain and copyrighted. Post-1970s, copyrighted.

FIGURE 10.1. Melies' *Trip to the Moon*. 1902. Early example of animated filmmaking. Footagesource.com

INTRODUCTION

Animation has grown from an experimental art form at the turn of the last century into a billion-dollar industry, with names like Disney and Pixar becoming standards in their own right.

Animated films were one of the earliest forms of entertainment, going back to the late 1890s. Filmmakers experimented with the camera and realized they could trick the audience by simply starting and stopping the camera and substituting images.

This chapter explores several types of animation used in film over the past century. These include:

- Trick photography
- Stop-motion animation
- Miniatures
- 2-D cel animation
- Digital animation

Each one of these forms of animation evolved quickly, and this chapter explores how the advances in technology altered the animated look and feel.

EARLY ANIMATED TECHNOLOGIES

TRICK PHOTOGRAPHY

The earliest films date back to the mid 1890s. Filmmakers almost immediately began experimenting with camera techniques that would alter the look and feel of reality. Possibly the most famous was George Melies, who first began creating fantasy-oriented films in 1896. His only tools were the control of the camera, hand-tinting frames of film and editing, but he was able to achieve remarkable results that have become iconic images of classic motion picture history.

STOP-MOTION ANIMATION

Another early form of animation was stop-motion. This involved taking an object and shooting one frame of film, then moving the object's arms or legs slightly, then shooting another frame, and repeating this process until the object has been advanced through a complete range of movement. After many clicks, the audience would think the object was actually moving.

Filmmakers began making stop-motion shorts in the late 1890s. This form of animation was used in the 1926 classic *Lost World* and a few years later in *King Kong*. Almost a century later, animator Will Vinton continued using stop motion in his Raisin and M & M commercial campaigns. Tim Burton, who studied stop-motion animation as a student, continued to use the process in several of his films, including *The Nightmare Before Christmas* (1995) and *Corpse Bride* (2005).

MINIATURES

In 1898, the American Navy ship *USS Maine* sailed into Havana Harbor and blew up. The event would help push America into war and troops going into battle became entertainment for millions at

FIGURE 10.2. *Creation.* The producers of *King Kong* created this screen-test to show they could combine live action and stop-motion animation successfully for the production of *King Kong.* Footagesource.com

America's penny arcades. Audiences wanted to see a war in action, and pioneer filmmaker J. Stuart Blackton did not let them down. He cut out a picture of the *Maine*, put it in a bathtub and, by blowing cigar smoke and tossing lit firecrackers, re-created the scene. Audiences thought they saw the sinking of the *Maine*.

Miniatures soon became part of the film-going experience, with the best miniatures fooling the audience. A six-foot-tall Godzilla destroyed a miniature Tokyo. The real King Kong was only about a foot tall. Set decorators used the power of film illusion to create inexpensive backdrops that looked like they fit the image.

2-D Cel Animation

J. Stuart Blackton would go on to run Edison's Vitagraph studios and become one of the first innovators in filmmaking. Among his other firsts was producing *The Enchanted Well* in 1900, considered the first animated film using frames of art that appear to create movement. The idea was simple. Begin to draw, click. Draw some more, click. After many clicks of the camera, upon projection you had an animated moving object.

He was soon followed by Winsor McCay, a cartoonist who also experimented with early cel-art animation. McCay made film history by releasing *Gertie the Dinosaur* in 1914. It was a short cartoon that was projected while McCay did a stage show, interacting with his friendly dinosaur creation—a combination of motion pictures and vaudeville. *Gertie* not only showed that animation could work well with live action, but it could entertain audiences and opened the door for motion-picture animators. *Gertie* is the best preserved of McCay's films—some of which have been lost or survive only in fragments—and has been preserved in the US Library of Congress's National Film Registry as being "culturally, historically, or aesthetically significant."

FIGURE 10.3. *Gertie the Dinosaur.* Winsor McCay, 1914. Earliest animated film featuring a dinosaur. Footagesource.com

SOUND . . . AND THE GOLDEN AGE OF ANIMATION

By the late 1920s animation studios began producing short programs with accompanying soundtracks that would appear at the beginning of film programs. Animated cartoon production became a huge industry, and a number of legendary stars first made their appearance during this period. Among the animated stars that came along were:

- Krazy Kat
- Betty Boop
- Popeye
- Bugs Bunny

When television began to appear in homes around the world, early morning shows on the weekend became a time to bring in the kids and show them cartoons. Starting with old cartoons from the '30s and '40s, studios eventually began to create new material with new animated characters. Studios learned that the money was not only in the cartoon, but in the licensing of toy products that popular characters would help sell.

In the late 1960s the cost of animation grew and producers began to "simplify" their Saturday morning shows, with stationary backgrounds and characters who only moved their mouths. This saved a substantial amount of money but made for years of truly forgettable animated shows.

Television-based animated characters are an area to be careful about. Many shows were not copyrighted at the time of broadcast. However, studios could go back many years later and copyright the show as a new work. In addition, if the characters were exploited for commercial reasons (e.g., toys), they have further trademark protection, especially in the area of uses in advertising.

COMMERCIALS

In addition to Saturday morning television series, animators began to produce a wide variety of commercial brands. From Frosted Flakes featuring Tony the Tiger to Will Vinton's dancing raisins, animated characters were often best able to bring humor and emotion to an otherwise uninspired product line.

DIGITAL 2-D AND DIGITAL 3-D

Pixar was one of the earliest pioneers in unleashing the power of digitally creating animated films. Cel art was replaced by software programs that allowed artists greater freedom in developing backgrounds and character movement. The era of cel animation was all but dead by 2000.

FIGURE 10.4. Burning of United States Capitol Building. Thousands of special effects visuals are available for licensing, saving producers the cost of creating artwork. Courtesy Mitchell Calhoun.

The ability to use computer programs has allowed animation to go to levels never imagined. Mixing 2-D and 3-D images, easily matching live-action characters with animated ones, plus cost-efficiencies, made the cartoons of today substantially richer compared to what was being produced from the '60s to the '80s.

☙ SUMMARY

Animation has been part of the film-going experience for more than 120 years. Thousands of cartoons, commercials, TV shows and feature films have used a growing technology that helped create the magical illusion that is animation.

Many of the older films produced prior to television are in the public domain. However, famous characters from these cartoons that were exploited as brands, like Popeye the Sailor and Betty Boop, are still protected for commercial use. All programs produced since the 1950s should be considered to be protected by copyright until proven otherwise.

CHAPTER 11

AUDIO RECORDINGS

- **Type of medium:** Audio. Various technologies.
- **Years in use:** 1875 to the present.
- **Audience:** Worldwide.
- **Copyright status:** Pre-mid 1920s, public domain. Afterward, mixed copyright and public domain.

❦ INTRODUCTION

The earliest recordings (1877 to 1925) were entirely made through mechanical devices. These used a large conical horn to focus the sound waves produced by the human voice or musical instruments. As the changing air pressure moved a diaphragm back and forth,

FIGURE 11.1. Wax recording player. Circa 1900. Footagesource.com

FIGURE 11.2. Graphophone advertisement with record. Footagesource.com

a stylus scratched an analog copy of the sound waves onto a roll of coated paper, or a cylinder or a soft wax surface. The quality of recordings was relatively poor, but it allowed for the first time recordings of music, speeches and events.

By the end of this era, disc recordings had become the standard and its dominance in the domestic audio market lasted until the end of the twentieth century.

THE ELECTRICAL ERA (1925 TO 1945) INCLUDING SOUND ON FILM

Sound recording's next major technological advance occurred when Western Electric introduced an integrated system of electrical microphones, electronic signal amplifiers and electromechanical recorders. This was soon adopted by most major US record labels by 1925 and the quality of sound recordings became markedly improved.

The recording technology was matched by the wider use of disc records, most notably the polyvinyl plastic discs that are still in use today.

FIGURE 11.3. NBC Radio Network west coast headquarters. 1950. Footagesource.com

SOUND ON FILM

Western Electric also introduced the sound-on-film technology in which the side of the film had an "optical audio track" that could be read and played at theaters. The film industry adopted this technology by the early 1930s and the era of sound films came into being.

❦ THE MAGNETIC ERA (1945 TO 1975)

After World War II, captured German technologies allowed companies in the United States to introduce magnetic tape that would record audio on a thin layer of polyvinyl. This allowed for recording sessions to save the music on magnetic tape and then "mix" tracks for a sound that never was available before.

Film production companies adopted magnetic recordings, and the Nagra audio recorder was modified to be in synch with motion picture cameras for capturing sound while shooting.

Audio home tape recording units became popular by the late 1950s and thousands of hours of audio magnetic recordings have survived in closets and archives around the world.

❦ THE DIGITAL ERA (1975 TO PRESENT)

The most current audio recording era is marked by the move away from analog recording into digital recording technology. Over the past twenty years, digital sound encoding—first perfected by Sony in the 1970s—was able to capture sound by means of a rapid series of samples of the sound. When played back through a digital-to-analog converter, these audio samples formed a continuous flow of sound.

Digital audio technology has been the predominant means of recording for music, feature films and television over the past two decades. Software like Pro Tools is used to do audio design for

FIGURE 11.4. Digital sound recording. Courtesy of Sophia Alexander.

motion pictures and television programs. Audio workstations are used to record and reproduce music recording sessions.

This is the technology that was first introduced publicly on CD recordings, DVD and Blu-ray and is now commonly available through streaming audio and video.

WARNING ABOUT DIGITAL MATERIAL

Digital technology is dependent on file formats and software and hardware. Over the past twenty years, all of these formats have been evolving. Many recordings from twenty years ago may not be reproducible today in their original recording file format. The most recent versions of software often cannot open early file formats.

Millions of files exist in outdated formats that cannot be opened anymore. However, computer recovery companies exist around the

country and specialize in recovering data. So, if you need information on a file that is not accessible at home, you might investigate
data recovery. Be warned, it is time-intensive and expensive.

DATA-STORAGE AND FILE-SHARING NETWORKS

As many of you know, large companies don't like their material
stolen and will prosecute site operators and even individual down-
loaders. Although infringement remains a significant issue for
copyright owners, the development of digital audio has had considerable benefits for consumers. In addition to facilitating the
high-volume, low-cost transfer and storage of digital audio files,
this new technology has also powered an explosion in the availability of so-called "back-catalog" titles stored in the archives of
recording labels, in which streaming services are categorized, radio
or on-demand. Streaming services such as Pandora use the radio
model, allowing users to select playlists but not specific songs to
listen to, while services such as Apple Music or Spotify allow users
to listen to both individual songs and pre-made playlists.

☞ SUMMARY

Audio recordings predate film and go back to the late 1870s. They
include music, interviews, sound effects and all matters of representing life around the globe.

The early material predating the mid-1920s is in the public domain.
Material produced after this time may or may not be public domain
and needs to be verified.

Besides the clearance of copyright, recent recordings may also
require performance clearances. When clearing famous name
brands such as the Rolling Stones or Beatles, be prepared to pay
substantial sums of money.

CHAPTER 12

BOOKS

- **Type of medium:** Print.
- **Years in use:** 6,000 years.
- **Audience:** Worldwide.
- **Copyright Status:** Mix of public domain and copyright.

❦ INTRODUCTION

Books are the oldest mass media device. They trace their origin back to over 5,000 years ago when the Sumerian civilization in Mesopotamia developed a written language. Over the next two millennia written symbols spread, conveying an ability to communicate by written means in nearly every region of the world.

FIGURE 12.1. *Tennyson; Art Edition.* 1895. Footagesource.com

FIGURE 12.2. Ancient Egyptian writing. Forsher Collection.

Ancient Egyptians wrote on papyrus scrolls. Mayans created codices using paper made from the bark of fig trees. Romans used a combination of papyrus, parchment and wax tablets. The downside was that all these were relatively expensive and literacy rates were very low. Technological advancements would slowly change this over the next 1,500 years.

❧ TYPE

Reproducing books by hand was the practice for almost a thousand years before the idea of using wood and eventually metal "type" was introduced. Printer Johannes Guttenberg is credited with publishing the first mass-produced Bible in the 1450s. The idea of mass production of written material became popular and within two centuries a wide variety of mass produced books became available to the relatively small literate members of society.

FIGURE 12.3. The Guttenberg Bible. Footagesource.com

For the next three centuries, the majority of publications were directed toward religious institutions, wealthy families and government record keeping. It would take an industrial revolution to bring books to the masses.

STEAM PRESS AND PUBLIC EDUCATION

Beginning in the early part of the nineteenth century, steam-driven printing presses allowed for a much larger run of books than previously possible. At the same time, literacy rates were increasing as basic elementary education became available to children and young adults.

Books soon became one of the earliest forms of mass culture. Authors such as Mark Twain (aka Samuel Clemens) and Edgar Allan Poe became famous in the United States and Europe through their series of popular books. Later, Jules Verne helped create the

FIGURE 12.4. *Strive and Succeed.*
Original copy of popular nineteenth-
century book, a Horatio Alger story.
Forsher Collection.

science fiction genre by writing imaginative stories about space and
time travel. Books had opened up a new world of understanding
society in ways never imagined before. Tennyson's poetry could be
shared by tens of thousands of readers in the comfort of their living rooms. It was a new age.

☙ HOW CAN YOU USE BOOKS AS ARCHIVAL MATERIAL?

Most books written before 1920 are in the public domain. That
means you can tell your own version of a Dickensian novel or your
own inspired version of *Frankenstein* or Jules Verne's *A Trip to
the Moon*. You must take care not to use as your source any of
the countless revisions or remakes of the author's original story,
which are themselves copyright protected as separate works. Mary

Shelley's *Frankenstein* is public domain, but if you use Universal Studio's "monster" makeup, that isn't public domain and in fact is protected via trademarks and copyright.

SUMMARY

Many public domain books also have illustrations that are in the public domain. Original publications can be used visually for creating a setting or telling part of a story. Thousands of books spanning the past several centuries are available for your use.

If you need material from a more contemporary source, you will need to receive legal permission. The penalty for using other people's copyrighted works can be severe.

CHAPTER 13

ARTWORK

- **Type of medium:** Various.
- **Years in use:** Earliest humans to present.
- **Audience:** Worldwide.
- **Copyright status:** Mix of public domain and copyright.

☙ INTRODUCTION

In 1939 archeologists in Germany explored a cave and found a human figure with a lion's head, carved out of mammoth bone. It turned out that this very early piece of human artwork was made

FIGURE 13.1. *Mona Lisa.* Leonardo da Vinci. 1517. Footagesource.com

between 35 and 40 thousand years ago. Every culture since has left images reflecting their religions, customs, fashions and foods.

For filmmakers, artworks offer incredible value. Nearly everything made over a hundred years ago is in the public domain. Nobody technically owns the intellectual property rights. This includes all the historic art we still have from Greece, Rome, Egypt, China and the Americas. You get the idea . . . an incredible amount of material. Most of it is free!

Let's look at what is available for free and what you will have to license.

✔ ANCIENT ART

We are lucky to live in an age where we have the benefit of centuries of research and curation of ancient art coming from all corners of the earth. Luckier, a lot of this material has been photographed and digital copies are available within a few clicks.

FIGURE 13.2. Art illustrations from a book published in the 1890s. Thousands of these books were published and are both affordable and readily available at used-book stores, antique stores or online. The art is in the public domain. Footagesource.com

This is invaluable to archival researchers. You may be working on a film that asks you to recreate a time period, or a non-fiction film you are producing refers back to a period of time and you need a visual to represent the narrative. You may need inspiration for a science fiction film that feels both out of this world yet familiar. All this comes from reviewing different cultures and their design aesthetics.

And it's all free.

🍂 INDUSTRIAL AGE

No matter what part of the world you lived in, art was an expensive proposition to own up to the early nineteenth century. You had

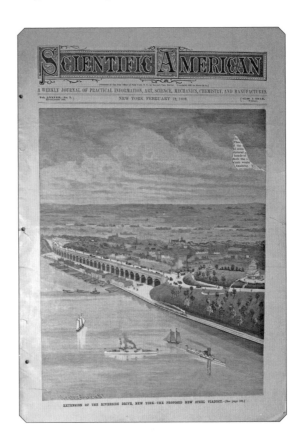

FIGURE 13.3. Early twentieth-century commercial art. Footagesource.com

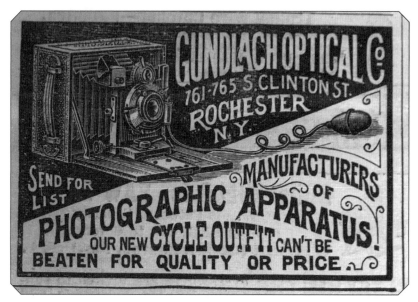

FIGURE 13.4. Early twentieth-century graphic artwork. Footagesource.com

to hire talented artists and pay them (unless they were slaves). In either case, commissioned art was limited to the affluent and only shared with the masses when they felt it appropriate.

Once the Industrial Age took hold, art became commercially accessible to the working class, too. Printing presses and steam engines allowed for mass reproduction of lithographs. Schools allowed the training of a larger pool of artists. An increasing middle class was able to afford to purchase art elements.

One major area where art took hold was in advertising. Advertisers soon realized that a print ad was not enough. They had to make their product look special. Thus was ushered in the age of commercial art. We have over 150 years of commercial advertisements, much of which can be considered in the public domain, with some major exceptions (see Part Three).

❧ MODERN AGE

Today, art is part of every aspect of our daily life. Art elements adorn the simplest web pages on our computer and cell phones. Books, CDs, DVDs and most every commercial item for sale has a "branding" that was developed by a commercial artist. Most colleges and universities have a fine arts department and millions of struggling artists are pounding away at creating their inspirations.

Unfortunately, just because there is an abundance of material doesn't mean you are free to use anything you choose. In fact, it is the opposite. Just watch any reality show on TV. The subjects walk into a room and a piece of art hangs on the wall. The chances are the editors and producer deliberately blur images in the background so that they are made unreadable.

Why? Artwork is protected by the same laws that protect all creative works. If you use an artist's work and you don't clear it, you are breaking the copyright law. In many ways, contemporary artwork may be one of the most complicated areas involving ownership rights (see Part Three). To clear contemporary artwork, here is a list of some of the people whom you might need to negotiate a deal with.

- ❧ Museum ownership
- ❧ Private collection ownership
- ❧ Photographer
- ❧ Artist
- ❧ Artist's estate

HOW ABOUT GRAFFITI?

Yes, even graffiti is protected. In 2018, clothing retailer H&M conducted a new media campaign for its "New Routine" sportswear, featuring a model back-flipping off a wall with graffiti in the background. The graffiti artist, Jason "Revok" Williams, recognized his artwork and his lawyer sent a cease and desist letter. This was followed by a social media campaign that painted H&M as art-ist-unfriendly when they said that this form of art could not be protected by copyright law.

The lesson seemingly learned is that literally any form of artistic expression today has a legal standing as a copyrighted work.

🌰 SUMMARY

Artwork spanning the last 39,000 years awaits your use. Finding representations of it is as easy as a few clicks on a search site.

Using the artwork requires some careful considerations. If you are using a photo of a museum piece, do you need to get the photographer's permission? Will the museum require their permission?

If it is a newer piece of art, you need to deal with the above issues as well as the artist's estate and private collectors.

CHAPTER 14

RADIO

- **Medium:** Audio.
- **History:** Entered popular culture in the early 1920s.
- **Audience:** Global.
- **Copyright:** Mix of public domain and copyright.

FIGURE 14.1. 1942. Radio show. Bob Hope and Betty Hutton perform for a radio broadcast to troops during World War II. Footagesource.com

❧ INTRODUCTION

After nearly three decades of experimentation, the first wireless radio transmission in the United States occurred in 1920. For the next decade, the device slowly gained popularity.

When radio was first introduced, many predicted the end of the record. Radio was a free medium for the public to hear music for which they would otherwise have to pay. While some companies saw radio as a new avenue for promotion, others feared it would hurt record sales and attendance at live performances.

Luckily, previous copyright laws already in place protected record companies, and radio stations soon had to negotiate paying a license fee for playing pre-recorded music through the American Society of Composers, Authors and Publishers (ASCAP), beginning in 1923.

❧ GOLDEN AGE OF RADIO

Radio came of age during the Great Depression and possibly due to the tight economic conditions became very popular. Ownership of radios grew from two out of five homes in 1931 to four out of five homes in 1938. Meanwhile, record sales fell from $75 million in 1929 to $26 million in 1938 (reaching a low point of $5 million in 1933).

With the growing popularity of radio, the broadcast networks NBC and CBS developed. Hundreds of regional stations also came along and helped connect communities in ways never before seen. It was also through the nationwide system of stations that the greatest musical talents were discovered, from Bing Crosby and Frank Sinatra to Elvis Presley and the Beatles. The horrors of

Figure 14.2. Family listening to radio. Living room, circa 1935. Library of Congress.

World War II were brought into everyone's living room each night and many of the first generation of television shows were introduced as radio programs that you could watch.

❦ FM RADIO IN THE AGE OF TELEVISION AND CARS

When Americans took to the roads in the 1950s, radio followed. By the early 1960s, the superior quality of the FM (frequency modulation) radio and its stereophonic output became part of most cars and teenage bedrooms. Radio was not displaced by television, but rather moved to cars, work environments and teenage hangouts.

☙ CONTEMPORARY RADIO AND THE INTERNET

Shortly after the year 2000, Sirius and XM took radio to the next level. They made their programming available both online and through satellites. In 2008, when they merged, the combined company offered subscribers over 100 channels. Since they did not broadcast but used either internet or satellite transmission, they offered a safe environment for talents like Howard Stern who was always facing FCC censorship and fines over the airwaves.

Today, all radio station models have changed to offer a website in addition to online and broadcast availability of their programming. As the internet's reach grew, the differences in what radio, newspapers and television websites offered began to erode.

They also allowed "time-shifting" viewing in which the programs were on servers and could be accessed anytime the viewer wished.

☙ USES OF RADIO FOR ARCHIVAL CONTENT

Thousands of hours of classic radio programming have been archived over the decades. News programs, dramas, comedies, musical hours and much more.

Many of these programs helped define the times in which they were broadcast. Radio programs during World War II delivered the emotional raw nature of a country fighting a formidable group of enemies. News programs from the Great Depression helped deliver what it was like to live in towns with nearly half the population unemployed. If you are producing a historic drama, nothing makes the scene more realistic than using an authentic radio program of the time your story takes place.

✿ SUMMARY

Radio programming developed during the 1920s and has consistently been part of the popular culture ever since.

Thousands of hours of radio programs that were recorded on vinyl still exist. Thousands of additional hours of radio programming were recorded when magnetic tape became popular in the 1950s,

These recordings tell the story of the past century. They include historic events, legendary actor interviews, music, comedy routines and theatrical presentations. This is material that can take an audience immediately to the time and place your script describes.

CHAPTER 15

A MILLION STORY IDEAS

- **Medium:** Print.
- **History:** Early newspapers go back to 1665.
- **Audience:** Global.
- **Copyright:** Mix of public domain and copyright.

❦ INTRODUCTION

Filmmakers are always looking to find a great story idea. That is
what is behind every great project. One treasure trove of literally
millions of ideas lies in archival print publications. Each day for
hundreds of years, thousands of papers and magazines published

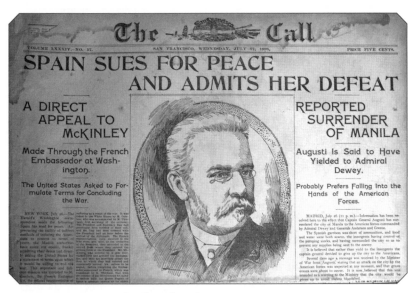

FIGURE 15.1. Newspaper headlines from the 1890s. Footagesource.com

countless interesting stories. The majority of these are waiting for you to find them.

These cover every possible subject. Scandals, romance, tragedies, war, fashion, technology. Whatever your particular interest area, you will find great material guaranteed to inspire a new interpretation of past events.

☙ MASS MEDIA AND THE BATTLE OF THE DAILY NEWSPAPERS

The first continuously published newspaper dates back to 1665 with the publication of the *London Gazette*. Papers made their way to the colonies in the New World and became part of most major cities by the mid-eighteenth century. Readership was limited due to the technological limitations of reproducing papers and the relatively small audience even able to read. That changed in 1833 with the introduction of the "penny press" when newspapers like the *New York Sun* began publishing larger runs, powered by steam presses. With a growing literate class, newspapers and soon magazines became common in most towns and cities around the United States and Europe.

By the mid-nineteenth century most cities had introduced penny presses and the literacy rate continued to increase. These papers were the source for national and local news and included advertisements, political announcements and domestic as well as international news stories. Newspapers and magazines had become the first mass media technology.

☙ MAGAZINE FRENZY

By the end of the nineteenth century, newspapers had grown to appeal to the entire population and included cartoons for the more

FIGURE 15.2. Newspaper featuring early use of photo print technology. Footagesource.com

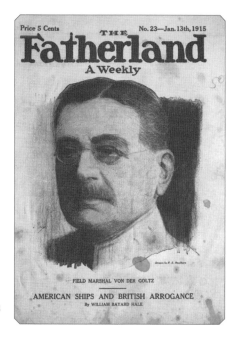

FIGURE 15.3. *The Fatherland Magazine.* World War I pro-German US magazine. Footagesource.com

youthful readers, sports, fashion, entertainment as well as news of the day. At the same time, hundreds of magazines began to be published and were available around the globe, covering a multitude of social and political audiences. Magazines like *Look* and *Life* would find broader audiences by the use of color photos and interesting stories, while other magazines were able to appeal to niche audiences.

☙ COMPETITION

Like all mass media, the number of daily newspapers across the country began declining during the mid-part of the twentieth century with the growing competition from radio and television. Audiences realized they heard news quicker on the radio instead of having to wait until the next morning's newspaper edition.

By the early 2000s, newspapers' very existence became threatened. Most cities lost their second newspaper, and those that survived faced shrinking revenue from classified advertisements, with advertisers realizing they could reach targeted markets much more affordably using the internet. Newspapers began to develop websites that would compete with local TV and radio stations.

☙ SUMMARY

Newspaper and magazine content from the 1600s to the 1920s is considered public domain. Newspaper content, advertisements and headlines are an invaluable source for research and graphics in your programming.

These are fantastic sources of inspiration for story ideas. Go to a library and ask to read their micro-fiche collection of newspapers and you will be both entertained and inspired.

WARNING: As has been said about other forms of archival material, one has to remain careful to get proper permissions from owners of any material a person or company can lay claim to. This might include banners and advertisements that may be protected by current trademarks, celebrity endorsements and showing a contemporary company in a less than favorable light.

FIGURE 15.4. Headline announcing death of Jefferson Davis, president of the Confederacy. December 7, 1889. Footagesource.com

CHAPTER 16

POSTERS & POSTCARDS

- **Type of medium:** Print.
- **Years in use:** 3000 BC to present.
- **Audience:** Global.
- **Copyright Status:** Pre-1920, public domain. 1920–1975, mix of public domain and copyrighted. Post-1975, copyrighted.

☙ INTRODUCTION

Posters are one of the oldest art forms. The streets of Pompeii still have examples of posters put up over two thousand years ago extolling gladiators and drinking establishments. Over the years, wall mountings have promoted cultural events, political movements and personal testimonies. The United States Civil War and the First World War had legions of graphic artists and propagandists working overtime to reach the masses. Posters are a treasure trove awaiting your discovery.

☙ MOVIE POSTERS

The tradition of movie posters goes back to the late 1890s and penny arcades. Short newsreels of the Spanish-American War became popular entertainment and penny arcade owners would create posters that described what the newsreels that day showed. When the films moved to nickel theaters, short films were often accompanied by movie posters. By 1912, when feature films came along and the star system became established, posters were part of every film presentation.

FIGURE 16.1.
The Outlaw.
Poster for Howard
Hughes' censored
feature film.
Footagesource.com

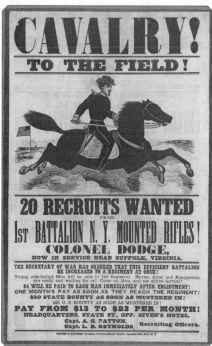

FIGURE 16.2. Civil War poster. Library
of Congress.

FIGURE; 16.3. Movie poster for *A Star Is Born* (1937). Footagesource.com

Today, tens of thousands of movie posters exist. They have become a collectors market, with many famous titles costing in the tens of thousands of dollars. But the great majority of posters cost only a few dollars and are readily available on sites like eBay. Many of these older posters contain artwork that is available with little copyright problem for use in current works (see Part Three).

~ SPOTLIGHT ON . . .

MOVIE POSTERS

ERIC CAIDIN (1952-2015),
founder of Hollywood Book and Poster Company

Forsher: Let's say you were going to give advice to people who are researching, doing a documentary. What's the first thing in terms of process that they should do to even figure out how to find paper print material?

Eric: It's actually so easy now. You can just go on the internet and you can basically do a search. You can actually find, you can locate, every single store in pretty much every city in the United States. There's actually quite a lot of stores that specialize with every type of collectible.

Forsher: What would be the key words that would get you in there?

Eric: I say probably "movie posters" right there would get you every store in the United States and into the world.

Forsher: How do they even figure out they need a movie poster in terms of finding material? You're a researcher, you're doing a documentary on Fay Wray or something.

Eric: Well, it's unlimited what you can get on every single actor, actress, TV show, film, whatever. I mean, when you go down the list and check with every store, every store is going to have different material. And the stuff is available for sale. You'd be very surprised at what is available. Some of the stuff's original material and will cost you quite a lot of money, but you can always get reproductions or copies at a very low price. You can find things, everything you'd want, at a very reasonable price.

Forsher: Can't you also negotiate, like if you don't necessarily want to buy it, but want to shoot it?

Eric: I'm sure there is. There's quite a lot of merchandise. Material, there's quite a lot to be rented. You know, the problem there is a lot of times the rent price will almost be the exact same amount of money as the cost of the merchandise. So, sometimes it's not really feasible to do that. Unless it's something really, really rare that you don't want to spend 15,000 dollars on when you can rent it for 1,500 to 2,500 dollars.

Forsher: What are rights issues related to paper stuff?

Eric: That's a little bit of a gray area there. Movie posters I don't think fall in the common market place. The movie posters you don't normally need permission to shoot because they are out in the market. The photos are a different story. You have to get the rights from the photographer, which is going to be almost impossible sometimes to track down, unless their name is on the photo. Or you have to get the rights to the reproduced photos from the individual studios that have the license and rights. That's something that has to be done. You can't just go and get some photos from a movie or a TV show, or a public figure and just basically put it in a book or magazine or anything without getting permission. Because they have the rights.

Forsher: Give me some range of very affordable types of paper print stuff as compared to outrageously expensive stuff that you've dealt with.

Eric: Well, at this point they've come out with reproduction posters of pretty much every class of movie and the poster prices range, depends on size of course, but they can go anywhere from eight dollars to twenty dollars. So you can go ahead and pick up a reproduction of a *Casablanca* poster for eight dollars, fifteen dollars, or twenty dollars. Which if you want to buy an original, if you could find one at an auction company, is going to cost you probably in the range of between maybe 50,000 to 75,000 dollars. Maybe even 100,000 dollars, or over. So, if the person is not a die-hard collector with a lot of money, they're going to jump in there and buy the reprint.

Forsher: Any other bits of advice you can give people in terms of using paper print?

Eric: Nowadays it's more accessible if you're doing a book or a magazine or even a film to do research and use materials because it's so readily available now, there's so many stores that make this available to the public, unlike the old days. If you're a collector though, it's a different story . . . unfortunately it's too late. Because, the prices for rare classic films are out of this world. If you look at the auction companies who do the movie poster auctions and look at other stores who have a lot of the older material, the prices have escalated now to totally . . . it's way beyond the means of any regular collector.

POLITICAL AND PROPAGANDA POSTERS

Persuasion goes back to the earliest forms of government. A royal portrait was often all that was needed to remind the masses who was in charge.

FIGURE 16.4. 1960 presidential campaign poster. Library of Congress.

Today, the same principle holds. Posters, T-shirts and hats are part of the battle for the hearts and minds. It may be a small city council race or a bitter presidential campaign, but politics is all about branding and demonizing. What better way to reach people on an intimate basis than a poster.

During wartime, posters help the propaganda effort, helping define the enemy as untrustworthy, animalistic or brutal. Thousands of posters can be found that give visual representation to both politics and conflict over the past three centuries.

❧ ADVERTISEMENT

Branding became very popular with the advancements in printing presses and lithography. Posters promoting brands could be found (and can still be found) on any wall that pedestrians and drivers frequent.

FIGURE 16.5. Advertisement from the turn of the 20th century. Footagesource.com

❦ WHY USE POSTERS?

They are a great source of inexpensive artwork. They immediately enrich your film and help tell your story. Most important is that an immense amount of this material exists. Why wouldn't you use this material?

Same story as the other forms of archival material. Even though older posters produced before World War II are usually very safe to use for visuals in your film, trademarks are closely guarded and if you use a trademark in a way that makes the trademark holder upset, you might get sued. Also, modern posters may feature models or famous film and TV talent. They are on the poster because they were paid, and they limit the usage to the original shoot, not re-use.

They are plentiful, often colorful and quickly tell a story. They feature stars, advertisements and politics. In other words, when you need transition visuals to help tell your story, poster art is one of the best and most affordable sources of visuals.

❦ POSTCARDS

With the popularity of mail and the technology of printing photographs, postcards became a popular medium to send greetings. Millions of postcards have been printed over the past 150 years and offer colorful examples of showing pop culture in unique ways.

Where can you find postcards?

The first place to look is your own family collections. Older family members will often keep postcards from other family members.

Postcards can be found at affordable prices on eBay and in almost every antique store, Goodwill or rummage shop. The collectors market for postcards has been shrinking, which means that you can negotiate a good price for all but the most unique items. These are usually very safe to use, but any postcards produced after World

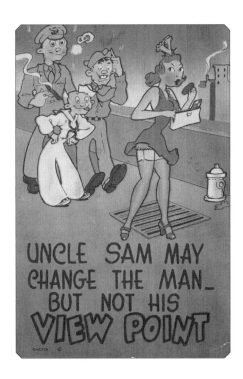

FIGURE 16.6. 1940s World War II
postcard. Footagesource.com

War II should be double-checked for publishers still in business
and monitoring their copyrights.

✿ SUMMARY

Posters and postcards are an affordable resource that can be used
in a multitude of ways in your media project. They have been in
common use for over 150 years and tell stories about almost every
aspect of our society.

Each section of this book has an assignment. These will give you the experience all filmmakers looking for archival material must go through to successfully find and access the material they might be able to use.

ASSIGNMENT ONE

Find an existing show or film concept. If you don't have one, write a page that describes a TV show or feature that you would like to produce.

Create a list of archival materials that might fit in with your idea. These might include stock footage, photos, art elements or museum pieces. If your story takes place in a specific time period, you might be looking at music from that time.

One hint is to remember that your visual background is the co-star. If your story is about a family from the 1980s, the background will include cars, fashions, artwork, and no cell phones but voice mail machines. This will require some research to make sure you get all the nuances that make your story come to life.

PART TWO

WHERE TO FIND IT

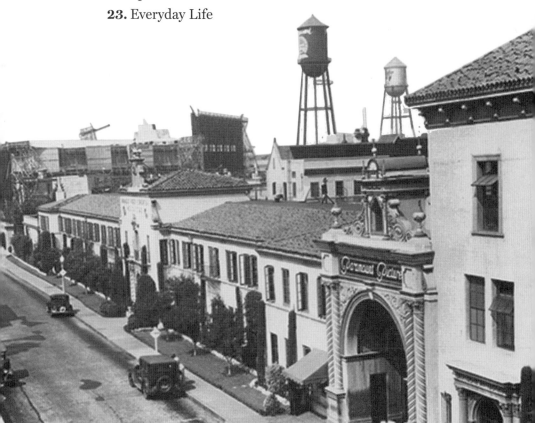

CHAPTER 17

MOST AFFORDABLE SOURCES OF ARCHIVAL MATERIAL

❧ INTRODUCTION

The best place to begin your archival hunt for material is where it will cost the least. This chapter looks at the key institutions in the United States that offer archival material without paying the cost of expensive copyright fees.

FIGURE 17.1. Inside the Footagesource film archive. Footagesource.com

You might be surprised to find that hundreds of thousands of hours of public domain material exists and is available to you. This includes feature films, newsreels, animated material, corporate and educational films, photos, graphics and, well, just about everything else.

The challenge is figuring out where to find it. The inexpensive material is primarily located in several key archives which are described on the following pages.

✇ NATIONAL ARCHIVES

The National Archives was established in 1934 as the nation's record keeper. By law, "permanently valuable" records of the federal government are required to go to the National Archives for safekeeping. This includes handwritten documents, maps, films and even email. The National Archives only keeps a small portion of the government output but this means that it has around ten billion records . . . and growing.

FIGURE 17.2. David Packard building, United States National Archives. College Park, Maryland. Courtesy of the National Archives.

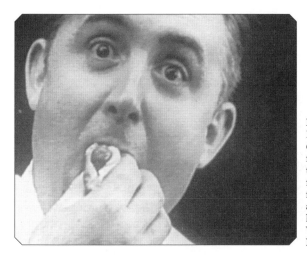

FIGURE 17.3.
Department of Defense
GI Quiz. Hundreds of
films were produced
to prepare soldiers
for fighting as well as
for reentering society
after the war. Eating
hot dogs was from a
World War II *GI Quiz*.
National Archives.

TYPES OF MATERIAL

The National Archives is undoubtedly the biggest collection of archival material in the United States. It has tens of thousands of sound recordings, millions of photographic items, and thousands of reels of motion picture film, and the collections continue to grow. It has the holdings of items donated by the departments of defense, agriculture, education, and other agencies.

Not only does it contain the rich resources of these government areas, but it also has some sizable donations that you need to know about. Among them are the Universal Newsreel Collection and the Ford Historic Film Collection.

UNIVERSAL NEWSREEL COLLECTION

Universal Studios donated its entire newsreel collection to the National Archives in 1976. The newsreel service was in operation between the late 1920s and 1967, turning out two issues a week. The collection not only includes the newsreels, but also a sizable collection of outtakes that didn't make the news. In addition, the collection has many public service announcements from the decades, featuring a wide assortment of stars promoting their favorite charity or cause.

A substantial part of the collection was destroyed in a fire several years ago but the collection still contains several thousand elements. For any show that contains historical footage documenting the twentieth century, this is your first stop.

WEBSITE—https://archive.org/details/universal_newsreels&tab =collection

COPYRIGHTED OR PUBLIC DOMAIN?

The National Archives substantially consists of material in the public domain. Having said that, there are some restrictions. These include documents that have not been cleared for viewing outside of research.

Government films also can be subject to specific restrictions. Often times they have licensed material within them that was limited to the original use of the film. It is your responsibility to be on the lookout and clear these. For example, years ago I secured a US government film on earthquake preparedness which focused on the Sylmar California earthquake of 1971. In this film was a brief excerpt taken from the MGM classic *San Francisco,* showing the destruction of the city. This film clip is copyrighted. Just because the primary film is in the public domain, it doesn't mean everything in it is public domain.

HOW TO ACCESS FOOTAGE

I encourage all readers of this book to go explore the holdings of the National Archives. It is an amazing place and by going you will get a much greater feel of what is available.

If that is impossible, you can hire a researcher. Reaching a private National Archives researcher can be done by going to the National Archives website and clicking on "Hiring a Researcher."

WEBSITE—https://archive.org/details/universal_newsreels

How Much Does It Cost When It's Free?

Plenty. In addition to research fees and any potential copyright issue, be aware that you need to pay for all duplication expenses for ordered material. This can add up, with film-to-tape or digital-format transfers costing in the hundreds of dollars per order.

FIGURE 17.4.
Henry Ford picnic.
Ford Collection,
National Archives.

Ford Historical Film Collection

Ford Motors donated a sizable collection of over 1.5 million feet of film to the National Archives in 1963. The Ford Historical Film Collection contains films about manufacturing, tours of cities, Henry Ford home movies and a wide number of interesting political and educational films they collected during this period.

This is a great source of footage for establishing images that say "Americana" from the turn of the last century to the 1950s.

Types of Material

The library contains footage from 1914 to the mid-1950s.

- Newsreels
- Educational films
- Classic home movies
- Government films

- Footage on technology
- Footage on transportation
- Footage on cities and rural America

COPYRIGHT INFORMATION

Films are in the public domain. Be aware of possible copyrighted material that may be found within films.

HOW TO ACCESS FOOTAGE

You can visit the National Archives and look at "desk copies" of many of the films. If you bring a recording device, you can make a copy of the "reference copy." Be forewarned that these are low-quality duplicates and not usable in your final edited project.

If you find something you like, you order it and pay the duplication fees.

You can also access the material by hiring a researcher and requesting a research report and a video viewing copy.

WEBSITE—https://www.archives.gov/research/guides/catalog-film-sound-video.html

⌒ SPOTLIGHT ON . . .

BONNIE ROWAN, Film Researcher

Bonnie is a veteran researcher who over the past fifteen years has specialized in finding material both in the National Archives and the Library of Congress. Her background before becoming a researcher includes working in film history and production.

She has put together some important advice that will help you in working with researchers and finding materials housed under these federal agencies.

- *Washington-area institutions hold the world's largest collections of motion pictures, stills, audio recordings and newspaper files.*
- *Many collections are unique and often rights-free.*
- *None are accessible in simple databases. Only portions of the holdings of the National Archives and Library of Congress can be searched online and each database has quirky problems.*
- *Ordering broadcast-quality copies is confusing and turn-around time is usually related to the skills of the person placing the order.*
- *Some institutions will answer research requests but these are low priority and often done under pressure by ill-trained staff.*
- *Inform the researcher as soon as you know anything about your subject.*
- *Searches for a list of images to match an already completed script can be accomplished but you have wasted the greatest potential of these vast collections. Work with the researcher at the idea stage!*
- *Use the online databases of the Library of Congress and National Archives but do it in consultation with the researcher. The online searches should be considered a starting-off point and not the end point.*

BONNIE G. ROWAN FILM RESEARCH
browan@his.com

NASA

The film library of the National Aeronautics and Space Administration (NASA) contains an enormous array of films detailing every era of flight, current space programs and futuristic flights created by animation. Their archives go beyond rockets and space missions and include films going back to the first manned flights with the Wright brothers starting in 1903.

FIGURE 17.5. NASA photo of a spacewalk. NASA.

TYPES OF MATERIAL

- Historical documentaries on the history of flight
- Footage of rocket launches
- Footage of astronauts, dating back to first manned flights
- Films about future space missions

COPYRIGHT INFORMATION

All films are in the public domain. Be sure to ask about any restrictions on use, including copyrighted material in films, music and graphic images. See Part Three about negotiating materials.

HOW TO ACCESS FOOTAGE

NASA has extensive image and video galleries online, including historic images, current missions, astronomy pictures, and ways to search for NASA images. Generally, each mission and program has a video and image collection on the topic page.

For example, space station videos can be found at https://www. nasa.gov/mission_pages/station/videos/index.html. Content can also be found on NASA's extensive social media channels.

For questions about specific images, call 202-358-1900. For questions about specific videos, call 202-358-0309.

WEBSITE—https://images.nasa.gov/
Restriction: The NASA insignia logo (the blue "meatball" insignia), the retired NASA logotype (the red "worm" logo) and the NASA seal may not be used for any purpose without explicit permission. These images may not be used by persons who are not NASA employees or on products, publications or web pages that are not NASA-sponsored. These images may not be used to imply endorsement or support of any external organization, program, effort, or persons.

STILL IMAGES, AUDIO RECORDINGS, VIDEO, AND RELATED COMPUTER FILES FOR NON-COMMERCIAL USE

NASA content—images, audio, video, and computer files used in the rendition of three-dimensional models, such as texture maps and polygon data in any format—generally are not copyrighted. You may use this material for educational or informational purposes, including photo collections, textbooks, public exhibits, computer graphical simulations and internet web pages. This general permission extends to personal web pages.

News outlets, schools, and text-book authors may use NASA content without needing explicit permission. NASA content used in a factual manner that does not imply endorsement may be used without needing explicit permission. NASA should be acknowledged as the source of the material. NASA occasionally uses copyrighted material by permission on its website. Those images will be marked copyright with the name of the copyright holder. NASA's use does not convey any rights to others to use the same material. Those wishing to use copyrighted material must contact the copyright holder directly.

FIGURE 17. 6. Library of Congress building, Washington DC.

☙ LIBRARY OF CONGRESS

The Library of Congress, established in 1800, is the world's largest collection of knowledge and creativity, with treasures in 460 different languages. The Library is constantly growing, taking in more than 10,000 objects a day.

As the nation's copyright repository, the Library receives two copies of every item registered for US copyright. It also operates offices around the world to bring in and distribute materials from other countries. Many of the Library's landmark objects and collections— such as the first map with the word "America" and the papers of Abraham Lincoln—have been donated by individuals or groups, or purchased using donated funds. The Library is an independent federal agency within the executive branch of the United States government.

The Library is a great place to locate free primary sources in a wide variety of media.

WHAT IS AVAILABLE

- ☙ Motion pictures

- Stills
- Historic documents
- Sound recordings
- Books

RESTRICTIONS

The Library of Congress is the repository for copyrighted works. That means that many items in the collection were and are still in copyright.

That being said, many of the items have fallen out of copyright and are usable. Your researcher can find this information for you when they are searching for material to fit your project.

HOW TO ACCESS MATERIAL

You can visit the Library and go through their research files. If that is impossible, hire a researcher to go through the collection.

One important resource of the Library of Congress is being able to give you the final word as to what is copyrighted and what is no longer copyrighted, or where no copyright exists. When you finish your personal research and have created a list of possible public domain titles, I suggest you send this list to the Library of Congress and request a research report. If they say it is in the public domain, and if somebody comes after you later, complaining you stole their film, all you need to do is send them the report and have them explain how they have a copyright when the Library of Congress says they don't. It will save you a lot of grief.

WEBSITES—

For more information about Library of Congress reports, go to https://www.copyright.gov/rrc/

For a detailed list of newspapers, go to https://www.loc.gov/rr/news/18th/

James Forsher Productions

-2-

A STAR IS BORN. Released by Warner Bros. Pictures.
182 minutes, sound, color, 35mm. CinemaScope.
Technicolor. Based on the Dorothy Parker, Alan
Campbell, Robert Carson screenplay, from a story by
William A. Wellman and Robert Carson. Registered in
the name of Warner Bros. Pictures, Inc., under
Lp 5396 following publication October 16, 1954.
Renewed under RE 136-425, September 1, 1982, by Warner
Bros., Inc., as proprietor of copyright in a work made
for hire.

THE RAY MILLAND SHOW. "A Star Is Born." 3 reels,
sound, black & white, 16mm. Registered in the name of
Revue Productions, Inc., under Lp 5712 following
publication October 28, 1954 (in notice: 1953).
Renewed under RE 97-311, July 29, 1981, by Universal
City Studios, Inc., as proprietor of copyright in a
work made for hire.

Our search in the Copyright Office indexes that include
documents cataloged through January 2, 1998 under the
names Revue Productions, Inc.; Seven Arts Associated
Corp.; Universal City Studios, Inc.; WBP, Inc.; Warner
Bros. Inc.; Warner Bros. Pictures, Inc. and Warner
Bros.-Seven Arts, Inc. and the titles THE RAY MILLAND
SHOW "A STAR IS BORN" and A STAR IS BORN disclosed
recordation of only the following document relating to
these works:

    FROM: WBP, Inc. dissolved (formerly Warner
               Bros. Pictures, Inc.)
    TO: Seven Arts Associated Corp., now known
               as Warner Bros.-Seven Arts, Inc.
    RE: A STAR IS BORN. L 5396 of 1954 & 210
               other titles. (Assignment).
    EXECUTED: April 15, 1968
    RECORDED: April 23, 1968
    IN: Vol. 1303, pp. 317-321

FIGURE 17.8. Library of
Congress research report.
For a fee, the LOC will
research to see if a film is in
the public domain or who
is the current copyright
holder. Footagesource.com

COPYRIGHT
OFFICE

February 9, 1998

James Forsher Productions
 Attn: James Forsher
 1600 Red Barber Plaza
 Tallahassee, FL 32310

Our reference: 98001592

LIBRARY
OF
CONGRESS

This refers to your letter of December 5, 1997.

Our search in the Cumulative Catalog of Motion Picture
Entries and the appropriate Copyright Office indexes
and catalogs that include works cataloged from 1946
through January 2, 1998 under the titles THIS IS
HOLLYWOOD (1950); MAX FACTOR (1950); JUNIOR PROM (1952)
and AMERICA THE AUTOMOBILE AGE (1962) disclosed no
separate registrations for motion pictures identified
under these specific titles.

Washington
D.C.
20559

Our search in the Cumulative Catalog of Motion Picture
Entries and the appropriate Copyright Office indexes
and catalogs that include works cataloged from 1912
through 1970 under the name Mascot Studios [Pictures
Corp.] and the title ONE FRIGHTENED NIGHT (1935)
disclosed the following separate registration for a
motion picture identified under this name and specific
title:

ONE FRIGHTENED NIGHT. Presented by Nat Levine.
(Stuart Palmer, author). 7 reels, sound. Registered
in the name of Mascot Pictures Corp., under L 5519
following publication May 6, 1935. No renewal found.

Our search in the Cumulative Catalog of Motion Picture
Entries and the appropriate Copyright Office indexes
and catalogs that include works cataloged from 1946
through January 2, 1998 under the titles {THE RAY
MILLAND SHOW} A STAR IS BORN (1954) disclosed the
following separate registrations for motion pictures
identified under the specific titles and bearing the
year date indicated:

FIGURE 17.9. Library of Congress document. Original Constitution of the United States. Library of Congress.

🌰 HOME MOVIES

One archival source most people ignore is right in their closets. Home movies and photo albums offer a treasure trove that captures the entire length of the past century. Home movies started to become popular in the 1920s, and by the 1950s most families could afford a basic 8mm camera to record vacations, holidays and school events.

In addition to your personal home movies, you have access to all of your family's and friends' materials, too. And if that isn't enough, you can go to almost any Goodwill store, antique mall or garage sale and find old films and videos that lived beyond the family that first created them.

ADVANTAGES OF HOME MOVIES
The biggest challenge to using archival material is the copyright costs and permissions. By using home movies and photo albums, you can approve the material because you own it or you can get your friends and family to do the same.

AND HOW ABOUT YOUTUBE?

As anyone who has suffered through a night of insomnia knows, YouTube has no end of videos. Millions and millions of film clips. Many look very old. Many look very cheap. All leading one to ask, why can't I use a clip from YouTube?

A few reasons. First, many of these clips are actually copyrighted. Media giant Viacom sued YouTube just over this reason. If it's copyrighted, it cannot be re-used unless you get the copyright owner's permission.

The second reason is quality. YouTube is a highly compressed video image. Some compressed videos are hardly watchable. You are not seeing the best quality image, even if it is public domain.

So, please use YouTube to research titles. Word searches are a great way to find films you never knew existed. Once you find material you would like to include in your show, do the research to figure out if a license is required and who has the best quality print.

☙ SUMMARY

Before hunting for footage at the studios and major archival houses, see what you can find that does not have copyright limitations. The government sources mentioned as well as your own family's and friends' media resources should give you an affordable head start in collecting the material you need.

Even with these affordable and available resources, always keep in mind that you want to pay attention to copyright laws. Part Three explores the dos and don'ts of conducting a solid copyright search.

CHAPTER 18

MAJOR STUDIOS AND DISTRIBUTORS

❧ INTRODUCTION

The Hollywood studio system dates back over 100 years to a time when a group of producers took advantage of the global love affair with motion pictures and began producing films like Henry Ford produced autos.

FIGURE 18.1. Entrance to Paramount Studios, Hollywood, California. Bison Archives.

The early studios were cities within a city. In addition to hiring hundreds of people to develop, write, shoot, edit and finally distribute a film, they had dentists, nurses, childcare, libraries, restaurants and all the requirements to keep an industry working around the clock.

A century later, all the original studios have streamlined their operations and have changed ownership several times. However, their large library of feature films, shorts, cartoons and behind-the-scene motion pictures are sitting in vaults and continue to have value beyond what their original producers could have ever imagined.

Added to the major studios are independent motion picture and television distributors. They serve the same function as major studios with one major difference: They do not have the real estate of a back lot. They are involved in financing and distributing films, often times owning the copyright.

LICENSING FROM MAJOR STUDIOS AND DISTRIBUTION COMPANIES

Studios have had a love/hate relationship with licensing their footage. In an era in which a major studio film release is expected to earn hundreds of millions of dollars or it's considered a failure, a division that brings in a million dollars is considered by some studio executives nothing more than a distraction and not worth putting energy into. Other more practical studio executives argue that a million dollars in profits is better than a film losing a million and are happy to work with producers. This is just a warning that many major studio clearance departments may not greet you with open arms.

❧ WHAT THEY GIVE YOU AND WHAT YOU STILL NEED TO GET

If you are lucky and secure a license for a film you want, be aware that you are only getting the rights the studio actually owns.

You will still have to get several other clearances. This is known as the four-union clearances. Starting in 1960, Hollywood guilds signed agreements with studios and producers that forced any re-users of films and performances to give creative talent additional payments.

Screen Actors Guild: Regarding any members of SAG/AFTRA (Screen Actors Guild/American Federation of Television and Radio Artists) appearing in film clips produced after 1960, you must ask their permission plus pay them a minimum of a day rate for their performance. But they might not want to give you their permission. Many years back, I did a documentary exploring censorship in Hollywood, with Peter Fonda as the host. I wanted to use a film clip from the film *Easy Rider*. The scene was Peter, Dennis Hopper and Jack Nicholson sitting around a fire and smoking a joint. I got the permission from the studio, Peter and Dennis Hopper. When I called Jack Nicholson's agent at the time, he informed me that "Jack doesn't participate in 'clip shows' and wouldn't sign off." Needless to say, we had to find another clip from the film.

Directors Guild: They do not have a right to stop your usage of the film clip, but you have to make a payment to the director.

Writers Guild: They do not have a right to stop your usage, but you have to make a payment.

Musicians Union: All musicians playing in the soundtrack must get paid.

Composer/Lyricist: You must negotiate a license fee. This may be a substantial amount of money. Recently I wanted to license the theme song from a 1960s television show for a documentary I was producing. The quote for non-theatrical rights from the music publisher was $10,000.

MAJOR COMPANIES AND WEBSITES

You can find contact information for most films and television shows on www.IMDbPro.com.

Here is a list of the largest studios and distributors:

- Paramount Studios/CBS
- Warner Bros.
- Universal
- Sony Studios
- MGM
- Lionsgate
- Twentieth Century Fox
- Focus
- Kingsworld
- Touchstone

FILM CLIP CLEARANCE FROM A MAJOR STUDIO

According to clearance expert James Tumminia, the common mistakes researchers and producers make primarily have to do with being realistic about marketplace licensing fees and terms, and scheduling. Many don't realize the costs of getting "grand rights" (all media, worldwide, in perpetuity) can be astronomically high and easily break a tight budget. Generally, I recommend licensing what rights are contractually needed (if grand rights aren't) and consider negotiating options for rights that may be needed later based on the budget. There are certain terms that can adversely impact an editor's creative style, too. Often, licensors charge a per-minute fee or have a minimum (e.g., 30 seconds). Many quick cuts from many sources would mean paying a lot more for a lot less than is being used.

The time it takes to get content licensed can vary and producers and editors must factor that in. This includes bringing a clearance professional on board as early as possible for a project that is heavy in licensable material so there is enough time to get quotes, negotiate terms, review and get mutually approved licenses and order master material. It may sound cliché, but the devil is in the details. Don't leave sourcing until the end; start the process right now. The internet is a great place to find audio/visual assets, but the copyright owner might not have or probably has not posted the asset. Finding who has the copyright could be time-consuming.

☙ LICENSING MUSIC

For most of the twentieth century, with the popularity of music on records, radio, film and television, a large number of music publishers were created who controlled the licensing of their collection of songs. This number has decreased somewhat over the past three decades with a small number of large companies having consolidated publishing rights, buying the rights to music compositions and lyrics.

When licensing music, make sure you are getting permission for both the words and the music. They are often separate rights, so don't assume you are getting both.

The first task is to find the current copyright holder. The rights to the song may have changed hands a dozen times since it was written and you want to be dealing only with the most current copyright holder or music publisher. You can find this out by going to the following sites.

The Music Publishers Association: http://www.mpa.org/content/copyright-search

ASCAP: ACE Database: https://www.ascap.com/repertory

The BMI: Repertory http://repertoire.bmi.com/StartPage.aspx

The search for music copyright owners is about to get a lot easier because BMI and ASCAP are creating a one-stop website to search ownership of music as part of the new copyright law. It should be online by the end of 2018. See this article for more information:

https://www.bmi.com/news/entry/bmi-ascap-announce-creation-of-new-musical-works-database

✿ SUMMARY

The major studios and distributors control the greatest number of feature films and TV shows. If you need a film clip from a film or TV show, you are very likely going to be dealing with one of the major studios or distributors.

I strongly suggest that if you need footage from a major studio or distribution company, hire a clip clearance specialist. They charge you an hourly or daily fee, but whatever you spend is a bargain and you get it back ten-fold.

Why? Because they have spent years nurturing relationships with the studios, music publishers and distributors. They personally know the players, what are reasonable fees and they know how to negotiate better than you will ever likely be able to.

Here is the scenario you want to avoid. You find yourself being charged a price you consider ridiculously expensive. You naturally start complaining about your budget and the next thing you know the studio clip clearance person on the other end of the line has hung up on you and won't return your repeated calls.

This is a classic example of the old saying, it's better to be penny-wise than pound-foolish.

CHAPTER 19

ARCHIVES

☙ INTRODUCTION

Most historic and investigative documentaries rely on footage to supplement the interviews. Even films firmly placed in the present often times need footage to establish different times and places. Luckily, hundreds of film and video archives exist that are full of this type of material.

FIGURE 19.1.
Video tape collection
of 1" tapes.
Footagesource.com

These archives don't specialize in major studio-owned feature films or TV shows with famous stars. Most have specialized collections with non-studio–owned features and every other type of media possible. ABC News Archives specializes in classic newsreels and contemporary news. Getty Images focuses on photographic and moving picture images. National Geographic has an exemplary collection of nature films and video clips.

Archival houses range from ridiculously inexpensive to the same prices as a major studio license fee. Over the past decade, they learned that the easier they make your job as a consumer of archival material, the more money they make. They often times have online search capability and can send links for the material, too. They all charge fees for screening cassettes and licensing fees for the master copy.

☙ PRIVATE FILM ARCHIVES

A large number of private film and video archives exist around the world. They are set up to preserve existing films and videos and make them available for licensing and research.

Technology keeps evolving, forcing archives to continuously change their database structures as new and better search options are created and brought to the marketplace. Don't be surprised to find a wide variety of search abilities as you go from archive to archive. Some may only be set up to create a viewing reel for you. Others will allow you to do all your own research online.

When you begin comparing the offerings of different archives, don't be surprised to find that many have similar or identical footage. This happens for a variety of reasons, but the most common is that various archives have large public domain holdings. They can charge whatever they can get away with and keep all of the license fee.

Don't hold this against them. Running an archive is expensive.

The large archives specialize in rare material not found in studios. These include interviews, documentaries, newsreels, cartoons, TV series that are not studio-owned and home movies. The largest archives such as Getty Images in the United States (www.gettyimages.com), INA in France (https://institut.ina.fr/en) and England's BFI (http://www.bfi.org.uk/archive-collections) are global concerns and invaluable resources. As large as they are, they still do not have every film or video and must be considered part of the search and not "one-stop" shopping.

FIGURE 19.2. Private archives specialize in rare interviews spanning a century of pop culture. Musician Frank Zappa talks about his fight against rock censorship in a 1987 filmed interview. Footagesource.com

⌒ SPOTLIGHT ON . . .

GLOBAL IMAGEWORKS

Global ImageWorks is a large archive that represents a wide number of filmmakers and archival holdings. This is how they describe their collection:

Tell your story with Global ImageWorks (GIW) footage and photos. GIW has the stock shots and the deep content you need to connect with your audience. Our extensive collection has been carefully curated based on our clients' needs.

Rights Managed • Royalty Free • Rights Ready • Premium Collections • Flexible Pricing • Free In-house Research

Highlights: Archival and contemporary footage and photos—Americana and nostalgia, destinations and travel, news and events, climate change, global conflict, pop culture and transportation. Celebrities, fashion, music and entertainment, rock 'n' roll and hip hop, science and technology, politics and history.

GIW's exclusive Premium Collections include the iconic television shows Austin City Limits *(1974–present),* The History of Rock and Roll Interview Archive, The Dick Cavett Show *(1968–1996),* Omnibus *(1952–1961), films of Robert Mugge and The Harold Lloyd Collection (1914–1947).*

The Global ImageWorks website offers a fully searchable online database with clips and photos available for viewing, online licensing and download . Enjoy our easy-to-use filters, user-friendly clipbins and lightboxes and free in-house research.

Footage supplied worldwide for documentaries, television shows, feature films, commercials, infomercials, museums, educational programs, music videos, video games, DVD supplements, web-based programming and other new media.

Other services: Global ImageWorks has an internationally recognized team offering research, rights and clearance services with over 35 years' experience in the industry. We offer footage and stills research, music and talent copyright clearances, consultations and planning, music and media supervision, and copyright administration.

WEBSITE—https://www.globalimageworks.com/

STATE FILM & PHOTO ARCHIVES

In addition to private film and video archives, many states have set up archives and make footage accessible to producers. These are often full of films that have some connection with the state they reside in. If you are interested in the history of Disney World, the State Archives of Florida has a great film on how the park was created. If you are studying civil rights history, the holdings of the Mississippi State Archive (http://www.mdah.ms.gov/new/) include thousands of documents, films and videos exploring the history of civil rights battles in that state.

State archives have their own research, licensing and duplicating costs which will be explained to you when you contact them. These will typically be less costly than private archive houses.

If you are producing a film that focuses on stories outside the United States, you will find a variety of archives in almost every country. Like US state archives, they all have different licensing and duplication costs, but they have material that is often unique to their part of the world.

LOCAL GOVERNMENT ARCHIVES.

One type of collection to try and locate is the photo collections of insurance companies. For many years, insurance companies photographed all the buildings they offered policies for. These collections were typically turned over to a state or local government for safekeeping, and offer an incredible amount of material spanning decades.

OFFICIAL RECORDS

Another truly amazing source of information is public records. These include marriage and death certificates, property purchases and the like.

The official records can provide documents that give your story a strong sense of reality. Figure 19.4 shows the death certificate of Marilyn Monroe, found in the public records at the city of Los Angeles. It tells you a story without having to say a word.

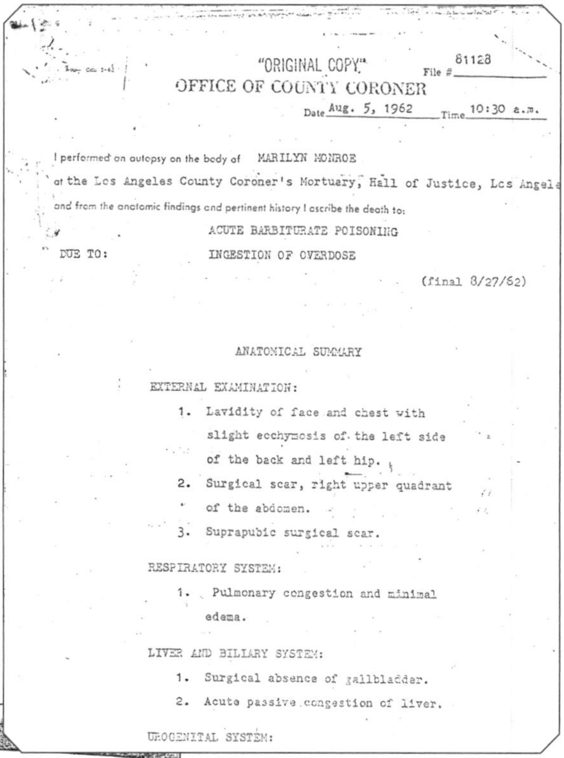

"ORIGINAL COPY"   81128
OFFICE OF COUNTY CORONER   File #

Date Aug. 5, 1962   Time 10:30 a.m.

I performed an autopsy on the body of   MARILYN MONROE

at the Los Angeles County Coroner's Mortuary, Hall of Justice, Los Angele

and from the anatomic findings and pertinent history I ascribe the death to:

ACUTE BARBITURATE POISONING

DUE TO: INGESTION OF OVERDOSE

(final 8/27/62)

ANATOMICAL SUMMARY

EXTERNAL EXAMINATION:

1. Lavidity of face and chest with slight ecchymosis of the left side of the back and left hip.

2. Surgical scar, right upper quadrant of the abdomen.

3. Suprapubic surgical scar.

RESPIRATORY SYSTEM:

1. Pulmonary congestion and minimal edema.

LIVER AND BILIARY SYSTEM:

1. Surgical absence of gallbladder.

2. Acute passive congestion of liver.

UROGENITAL SYSTEM:

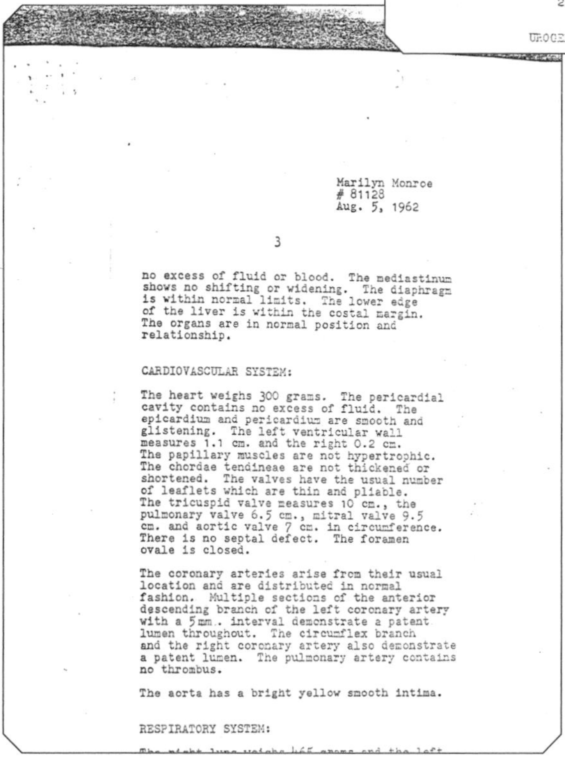

Marilyn Monroe
81128
Aug. 5, 1962

3

no excess of fluid or blood. The mediastinum shows no shifting or widening. The diaphragm is within normal limits. The lower edge of the liver is within the costal margin. The organs are in normal position and relationship.

CARDIOVASCULAR SYSTEM:

The heart weighs 300 grams. The pericardial cavity contains no excess of fluid. The epicardium and pericardium are smooth and glistening. The left ventricular wall measures 1.1 cm. and the right 0.2 cm. The papillary muscles are not hypertrophic. The chordae tendineae are not thickened or shortened. The valves have the usual number of leaflets which are thin and pliable. The tricuspid valve measures 10 cm., the pulmonary valve 6.5 cm., mitral valve 9.5 cm. and aortic valve 7 cm. in circumference. There is no septal defect. The foramen ovale is closed.

The coronary arteries arise from their usual location and are distributed in normal fashion. Multiple sections of the anterior descending branch of the left coronary artery with a 5 mm. interval demonstrate a patent lumen throughout. The circumflex branch and the right coronary artery also demonstrate a patent lumen. The pulmonary artery contains no thrombus.

The aorta has a bright yellow smooth intima.

RESPIRATORY SYSTEM:

The right lung weighs 465 grams and the left

FIGURE 19.4. Marilyn Monroe death certificate. City of Los Angeles. Footagesource.com

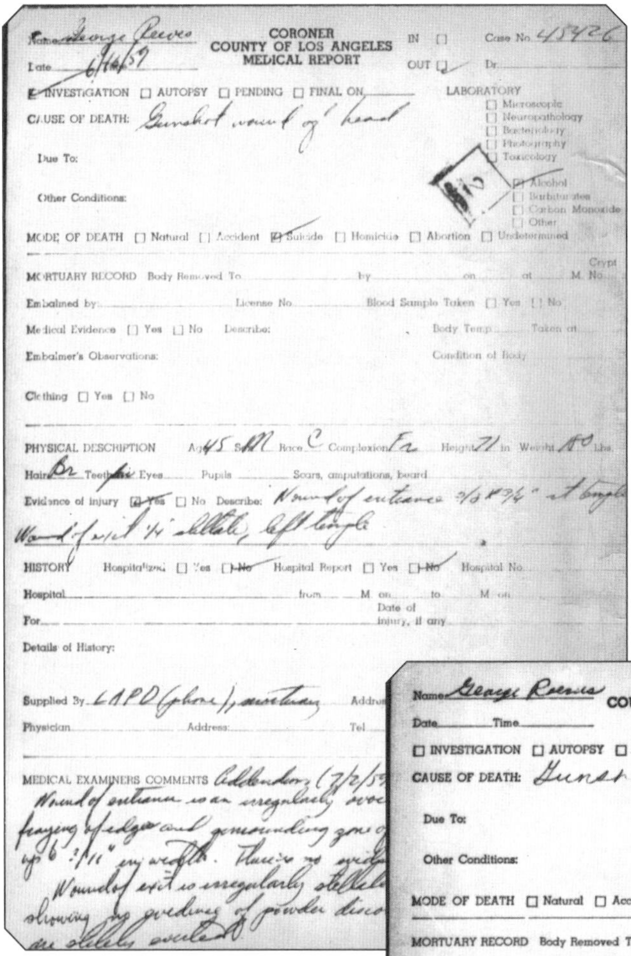

Name George Reeves — CORONER COUNTY OF LOS ANGELES MEDICAL REPORT — IN ☐ OUT ☐ — Case No. 45426

Date 6/16/59 — Dr.

☐ INVESTIGATION ☐ AUTOPSY ☐ PENDING ☐ FINAL ON

CAUSE OF DEATH: Gunshot wound of head

Due To:

Other Conditions:

LABORATORY ☐ Microscopic ☐ Neuropathology ☐ Bacteriology ☐ Photography ☐ Toxicology ☐ Alcohol ☐ Barbiturates ☐ Carbon Monoxide ☐ Other

MODE OF DEATH ☐ Natural ☐ Accident ☒ Suicide ☐ Homicide ☐ Abortion ☐ Undetermined

MORTUARY RECORD Body Removed To ___ by ___ on ___ at ___ M. Crypt No.

Embalmed by: ___ License No. ___ Blood Sample Taken ☐ Yes ☐ No

Medical Evidence ☐ Yes ☐ No Describe: ___ Body Temp. ___ Taken at

Embalmer's Observations: ___ Condition of Body

Clothing ☐ Yes ☐ No

PHYSICAL DESCRIPTION Age 45 Sex M Race C Complexion Fr Height 71 in. Weight 180 Lbs.

Hair Br Teeth fair Eyes ___ Pupils ___ Scars, amputations, beard

Evidence of injury ☒ Yes ☐ No Describe: Wound of entrance 3/8 x 3/4" rt temple

Wound of exit 1/4" stellate, left temple

HISTORY Hospitalized ☐ Yes ☒ No Hospital Report ☐ Yes ☒ No Hospital No.

Hospital ___ from ___ M. on ___ to ___ M. on

For ___ Date of injury, if any

Details of History:

Supplied By LAPD (phone), mortuary Address

Physician ___ Address: ___ Tel

MEDICAL EXAMINERS COMMENTS Addendum (7/2/59)

Wound of entrance is an irregularly ovo... fraying of edges and surrounding zone of ... up to 3/11" in width. There is no evid... Wound of exit is irregularly stellate... showing no evidence of powder disco... are slightly everted.

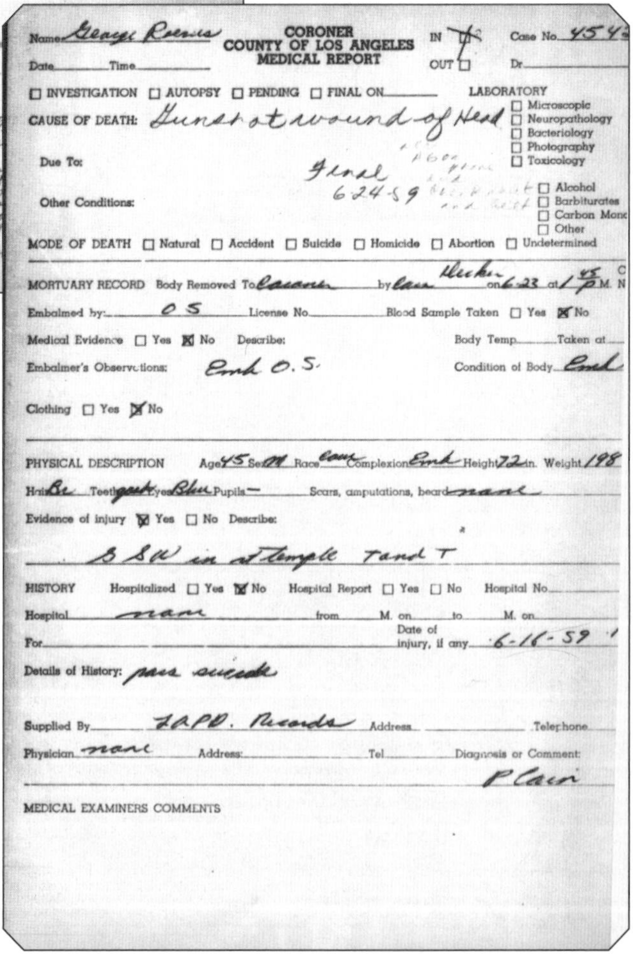

Name George Reeves — CORONER COUNTY OF LOS ANGELES MEDICAL REPORT — IN ☒ OUT ☐ — Case No. 454...

Date ___ Time ___ Dr.

☐ INVESTIGATION ☐ AUTOPSY ☐ PENDING ☐ FINAL ON

CAUSE OF DEATH: Gunshot wound of Head

Due To: Final 6-24-59

Other Conditions:

LABORATORY ☐ Microscopic ☐ Neuropathology ☐ Bacteriology ☐ Photography ☐ Toxicology ☐ Alcohol ☐ Barbiturates ☐ Carbon Monoxide ☐ Other

MODE OF DEATH ☐ Natural ☐ Accident ☐ Suicide ☐ Homicide ☐ Abortion ☐ Undetermined

MORTUARY RECORD Body Removed To Caccone by Lane Decker on 6-23 at 1:45 P.M.

Embalmed by: OS License No. ___ Blood Sample Taken ☐ Yes ☒ No

Medical Evidence ☐ Yes ☒ No Describe: ___ Body Temp. ___ Taken at

Embalmer's Observations: Emb O.S. — Condition of Body Emb

Clothing ☐ Yes ☒ No

PHYSICAL DESCRIPTION Age 45 Sex M Race Cau Complexion Emb Height 72 in. Weight 198

Hair Br Teeth good Eyes Blue Pupils — Scars, amputations, beard none

Evidence of injury ☒ Yes ☐ No Describe:

GSW in rt temple T and T

HISTORY Hospitalized ☐ Yes ☒ No Hospital Report ☐ Yes ☐ No Hospital No.

Hospital none from ___ M. on ___ to ___ M. on

For ___ Date of injury, if any 6-16-59

Details of History: poss suicide

Supplied By LAPD. Records Address ___ Telephone

Physician none Address: ___ Tel ___ Diagnosis or Comment: P Clair

MEDICAL EXAMINERS COMMENTS

FIGURE 19.5. Coroner report on George Reeves, TV's Superman. Footagesource.com

PRIVATE PHOTO ARCHIVES

Still photograph collections can be a tremendous and affordable tool in creating a show. The most affordable photo collections are in your own family's or your friends' family album collections, and with any luck, several generations of photos can exist in these family "archives." These are the best places to first look for historical still photos. They are free, one doesn't generally worry about clearances, and relatives can give some indication about who is in the photo, where it was taken and any other history.

LARGE COLLECTIONS

Starting with the most affordable, "buy-out" photo collections on CDs have become very common. The idea is simple. A company puts together hundreds —if not thousands—of photographs on a CD and charges you a flat fee. Once you buy their disk, it is free for you to use in any way you see fit (thus the term "buy-out" or royalty-free). The downside of buy-out photo collections is that while one gets a lot of volume, one may not get the photo that is really needed for your project. The more discerning the researcher, the less useful the CD.

Then there are the public domain government still photograph collections. At the federal level, the National Archives has millions of photos dating back to the Civil War era and covering numerous aspects of Americana, including government operations, American enterprise, agriculture, war, social concerns and health. State governments such as Florida have accessible photographic archives also. These usually relate to images pertinent to the region, but give a good cross-section of images of American life that often span physical boundaries. City and county governments also may have public domain collections that are available for a nominal fee.

If you cannot find what you are looking for in the public domain, the next stop is the private archives. They are often non-profit and usually associated with a university or historical group, but still charge fees for accessing and licensing. These collections are often tied to themes such as regional history or race or ethnic groups. By discovering what is in the collection, one can either dismiss it quickly or yell *bull's-eye*.

If all else fails, one can try the private photographic collections. Companies like Bison Archives specialize in Hollywood imagery. Larger companies like Getty Images specialize in having huge collections that feature famous photographers and a large subject breakdown to choose from. The advantage is that one is likely going to find the exact image. The downside is the relatively expensive licensing fees.

✿ PAPER COLLECTIONS

Paper collections refer to archives composed of printed (i.e., non-photographic) materials. These include newspapers, magazines, business records and printed artwork.

One area that has become a favorite collectors market over the past two decades is movie posters. Beginning at the turn of the century, films were promoted by advertisements that hung at the entrance to the theater, and those that have survived the years are prized by collectors. They also are a great medium to tell about a film and the society it was shown in (see chapter 16).

Getting your hands on posters requires a little investigation. You can try to find poster collectors through sites like www.ClassicImages.com. A more affordable way is to look on eBay or Amazon and search the title of the film poster you want. Many classic films have had their posters reproduced and can be purchased for a few dollars. Other titles that are not famous have original posters for sale that are affordable.

AUDIO LIBRARIES

Another specialized archive focuses on audio recordings. Several types of recording material exist at these archives.

- Musical recordings from the 1880s to the present
- Radio shows from the 1920s to the 1950s
- News reports

The first places to look include the Library of Congress, NASA and your local state archives. Private audio libraries include www.history.com that has speeches and other historical audio elements available online.

NEWSPAPERS AND MAGAZINES

Headlines are often used in non-fiction shows as an affordable and effective way to communicate a time and place. Newspaper and magazine stories offer a tremendous tool in both researching your story and supplying graphics that help tell your story.

Thousands of papers throughout the world publish stories daily that are ripe with drama. They become the inspiration not only for dramatic films and television shows, but documentaries, too. Many Hollywood production companies have employees that search out interesting stories to tie into their documentaries, films or TV shows. One can find newspaper stories in your own community, or use a search engine on the internet to find stories in other communities around the world

Magazines often focus on specific interest groups. They allow you to narrow a search for a topic by the type of audience the magazine appeals to. They also help one figure out the audience. The stories, whether historical or contemporary, need to be researched for ownership the same as stories you would uncover in a paper. Are they public domain or will you need permissions to tell the story?

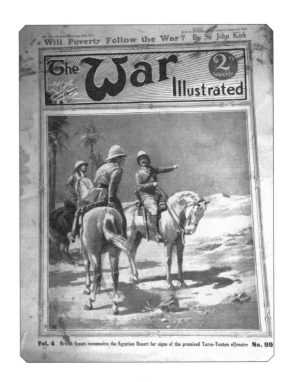

FIGURE 19.6. *The War* magazine, circa1917. Footagesource.com

Most newspapers have archival collections (often referred to as their "morgues"). Many of their older copies have been put on microfilm. As newspapers have gone out of business, their archives have either been donated to libraries, colleges, historical societies or, sadly, trash cans.

Magazines have suffered the same fate as newspapers, but with some perseverance, you can find a substantial number of existing copies of out-of-print issues.

If you need headlines, before calling the magazine or newspaper, you might want to talk with your local library's reference person. Many old newspapers and magazines have been put onto microfilm. You can make copies of these headlines and often not have to worry about license fees or expensive duplication costs.

FIGURE 19.7. Anti-weed movie poster. Forsher Collection.

🌿 PRODUCERS

Many films have been produced over the years outside of the Hollywood studio system. In the early days they were made by small production companies and screened in a "road show" manner by which a promoter would go to a town with an often exploitively titled film, put up a lot of posters, show the film over the following weekend and move on to the next town before anyone could ask too many questions.

Over the past three decades, independent films have tackled social, political, and racial topics in addition to being simply exploitive in nature. Some have fallen into the public domain but others still have copyrights kept by the producer or their heirs.

The challenge is to find the producer and see if they would be willing to license the rights to their film.

If you find an obscure film you must have in your project, I suggest you begin by conducting a Library of Congress copyright research report. Many of these films have had their copyright sold one or more times, and you don't want to give money to a less-than-honorable producer who forgot to mention to you that he sold all rights to his biker movie to another company in Japan back in the year 2000.

⟍ SPOTLIGHT ON . . .

Bison Archives

- **What are the steps a researcher should take before contacting you?**

When someone needs some research done they would email me informing me of what the project is, what exactly are they researching and asking me if I can help or not.

- **How do researchers negotiate use of a photo from Bison Archives?**

It depends on the use of the photo. If a student or non-profit needs the photo, I charge a "use fee" that they can afford. If it is a more professional "use" like a film company, magazine, newspaper, TV show, etc., then there are open-market prices that are charged. For example, the photo stock library Photofest in New York would charge a company from $75.00 and up depending on the use. The Getty Images Library would charge two to three times that amount for most projects.

- **What legal issues do you warn archival researchers about when licensing a photo?**

Generally most photographs are in the public domain, meaning that there is no copyright on the photo and most anyone can use it for most any project including a commercial use. A researcher would have to follow "due diligence," which means exhaust all sources to see if anyone might have a claim to the photograph. A detailed search list must be done to prove that the researcher tried to find a copyright holder. Most photographs which are in the public domain can be used within the "fair use" law, which means that it can be reasonably used for print publications (books and magazines and newspapers, etc.), but when a commercial use is needed, a researcher would have to make sure the photo is in the public domain and make sure that if there are people in the photo, they are not celebrities, etc., because if you used the photo for an advertisement, the celebrity could sue for money having their image used to exploitative purposes.

MARC WANAMAKER,
Bison Archives

❧ WHERE TO BEGIN: THE DIRECTORIES

A number of local, state and national entertainment industry directories exist like the Variety 411 (www.variety411.com) that offer hundreds of contact phone numbers and web pages to archives, research groups and dozens of other industry-related services. These are invaluable resources.

❧ SUMMARY

Numerous archives and collections exist around the world. They range from extremely affordable to extremely expensive, but they offer material not available in major studio collections nor at the National Archives or Library of Congress.

The key to working with any archive is to have done your preliminary research and know the exact type of footage, stills, newspaper stories or audio recordings they offer. They will dig into their collections and it is in their financial interest to find material you need, let alone come up with material you never dreamed even existed.

Which means you might have to start figuring out how to expand your budget projection.

CHAPTER 20

MUSEUMS & LIBRARIES

🍂 INTRODUCTION

Years ago I produced a show for the Discovery Channel about dino-
saurs and how they were portrayed in the movies. I had a very
limited budget but I wanted a visually rich environment in which
the host of the show would be tied to the theme. Luckily, I lived in
Los Angeles, home of the Los Angeles Natural History Museum and
their wonderful collection of dinosaur fossils. A couple of phone
calls later we had a million-dollar set for a modest location fee.

FIGURE 20.1. American Museum of Natural History, New York. Courtesy of the American
Museum of Natural History.

FINDING MATERIAL FOR YOUR STORY

Museums are a gold mine of information and resources, and they are plentiful. There are an estimated 50,000 museums around the world. You can start to find the museums that have material appropriate to your projects by an internet search using "museum" and keywords tied to your area. Wikipedia has a sizable list of links to a number of museums located around the world. You can also go to your local library and look at resource books that describe museums and their holdings.

So what can you find? Almost everything. If you are doing a project that tells the story of immigrants, you might want to contact the Lower East Side Tenement Museum in New York. They have re-created living conditions of immigrants who settled in their neighborhood over the years. If you are doing a project on mass shootings in America, several museums have put together exhibits focusing on mementos of grief.

Museums can offer you a tremendous amount of added value for your project. In addition to their holdings—the great majority of which are hidden in vaults and not seen by the public—they have environments that make great backdrops for shooting "b rolls" (establishing shots without talent) and host standups. Museums also employ experts that can serve as your experts for shows.

TYPES OF MUSEUMS

- Art
- Natural history
- Local and regional history
- Film and video
- Music and pop culture
- Ethnic and racial
- Science
- University museums

❦ WHAT YOU CAN FIND BEYOND THE EXHIBITS

RESEARCH COLLECTIONS

The great majority of holdings in most museums are in their vaults. Museums receive donations throughout the year and also acquire objects that fit into their core mission. Only a small fragment of these objects ever make it to the display case.

You will need to do the preliminary research to find which museum has the holdings that are appropriate for your projects. Your research quest may look something like this:

1. Decide what you are looking for.
2. Using keywords, do an internet search using several different search engines and see what institutions come up.
3. Figure out in what geographical part of the world your quest is centered and find out the museums located there. Contact them with an inquiry and see if they have any holdings that fit.

ACCESSIBLE HOLDINGS IN PUBLIC AND PRIVATE LIBRARIES

Some libraries make portions of their holdings accessible. They offer copies of films in their collections, reproductions of classic artwork and reprints of historic documents. Check with each institution if they require any special "re-use" license.

Libraries with specialized content may also include research libraries. You should inquire if you can get access to do research and possibly check out titles from the front desk.

A couple of years ago I produced a documentary on *Star Trek* producer Gene Roddenberry and his fight against censorship and segregation in Hollywood. My research took me to the UCLA library and a special collection that included all of his personal papers. It was a treasure trove showing his daily fight against

Figure 20.2. Shooting host in lobby of LA Natural History Museum for the Discovery Channel special *Hollywood Dinosaur Chronicles*. Forsher Productions

the network to get his vision of the world of the future on 1966 television.

TALKING WITH THE CURATOR

After you have researched your projects enough to know the general history of your topic, it is invaluable to find experts that have spent years studying your topic and can guide you to objects and information that you had no idea even existed.

Museum curators are often that type of expert. They know a tremendous amount about their chosen field and can be great subjects for interviews as well as your all-around point person for questions that come up.

❧ SUMMARY

Museums and libraries can offer you a variety of potential help. They may serve as an ideal backdrop to your host standup or dramatic scenes. Collectively, they offer an endless amount of objects that might fit into your production and, finally, experts that will help you tell your story.

Over the years that I have worked with large and small museums from coast to coast, I can't remember once any museum staff member not helping me with my requests.

CHAPTER 21

TELEVISION STATIONS

☙ INTRODUCTION

There are over 3,000 broadcast television stations around the United States, with thousands more in almost every country in the world. That is a lot of TV stations and they all have archival content.

Television began to reach audiences in noticeable numbers after World War II, growing phenomenally during the early 1950s. Every station began offering news programs in which local events were shot on film and rolled into the evening's local report. In the 1970s,

FIGURE 21.1. Television station production, 1946. Footagesource.com

film began to be replaced by videotape and the news divisions grew from fifteen minutes to an hour or longer each day.

If you need footage that documents events tied to a geographical area that took place after World War II, contacting the news division of television stations is a good initial call.

❧ LOCAL STATIONS

Local stations offer several types of archival material. These include:

News Packages: Cameramen and reporters went into the community and shot stories reflecting the big events of each day. These include natural disasters, murders, sports, scandals, and personal interest stories.

News Programs: Kinescopes and tapes exist of early news programs. These include full stories detailing the day's events, sports updates and weather reports.

Commercials: Many stations still have the original commercials or have them included in their old archival copies of shows.

Locally Produced Shows: Many stations produced public affairs and children's programming over the decades.

❧ NETWORKS

Television networks created prime-time programs for the stations they owned and their affiliates. During the 1950s they also owned much of their content. Copies of these network-owned shows may still exist in the network archives.

In the early 1960s, the federal government made the networks purchase programming from producers, breaking the monopoly they had enjoyed for the first twenty years of networks. These standards were relaxed over the past two decades, so there is no easy way to find out the copyright holder for network-aired programming. To secure licensing of most shows produced after 1960, check IMDb-Pro.com and the Library of Congress for current copyright holders.

~ SPOTLIGHT ON . . .

FOOTAGE.NET

DAVID SEEVERS, *Chief Marketing Executive at Footage.net explains how his archival resource site operates.*

Footage.net works with the world's leading footage companies to make their collections searchable on the Footage.net website. Footage.net makes it easy for creative professionals to search multiple

FIGURE 21.2. Footage.net is a website that provides filmmakers a single site to find numerous archives. Photo courtesy Footage.net.

footage collections simultaneously, access over 10 million records, view over 3.5 million clips and find the perfect shot.

The Footage.net search engine is free to use, and creative profession-als of all kinds use it to conduct thousands of searches per week. Footage.net is also home to Zap Email, which allows footage cus-tomers to send their footage requests to over forty of the world's top footage providers simultaneously.

Zap Email is a great way to get a footage search started, and an indispensable tool for unearthing hard-to-find shots.

❦ WHAT HAVE THE TELEVISION STATIONS KEPT?

During the 1950s and 1960s, many television stations and net-works faced a shortage of space to store their growing vaults full of programs. The easiest solution was to throw away old shows they didn't see much use in holding onto. Film collectors today own thousands of prints of shows that trace their existence back to resourceful rummagers going through trash bins in back of the network buildings.

Another source for these shows is the Library of Congress. Many program producers legally copyrighted their work by submitting a copy to the Library of Congress.

Finding an old show may not be as simple as you would think. One problem is that the shows are sometimes copyrighted in names that may not be the same as the show was called when it first aired. Years back I used a TV clip from *The Abbot and Costello Show* from the early 1950s. It was a Halloween show where the two comedi-ans walked through a haunted house and the episode had a title reflecting this story. We did a Library of Congress search and it showed that it had not been copyrighted. After the show aired, the Abbot and Costello estate attorney called our attorney and after a few discussions we found out that the episode was actually copyrighted as *The Abbot and Costello Show* followed by an episode number. The lesson I learned is that you really can't be too careful, but doing your due diligence will allow you to avoid the charge of malice and a costlier settlement.

Other TV stations have donated their old holdings to private or state archives. The TV stations you need material from will know who the recipient was and what years it covers.

✿ WHAT DO YOU GET WITH A LICENSE AGREEMENT FROM A NETWORK OR TV STATION?

Once you can locate the owner of the footage, you will get a license that allows you to use the footage in your show. If the program was produced after 1960, you will also be responsible for the same additional clearances you would need for a film: actors, writers, directors and music.

You may need to get additional clearance depending on the use. For example, if you find a TV show in which Elvis Presley appears, and you want to use this for a commercial you are producing, you will need to get permission from Elvis Presley Enterprises for using his likeness and performance.

✿ TRACING THE RIGHTS OF A SHOW. IT GETS COMPLICATED.

STAR TREK STORY

In 2015 I produced a documentary exploring the television career of producer Gene Roddenberry and the creation of *Star Trek*. We decided to include a clip from an early 1960s episode of *Star Trek*

FIGURE 21.3. Crew of *Star Trek* show at launch of the space shuttle USS *Enterprise*. From the documentary *Roddenberry's Trek*. Photo courtesy NASA.

in the documentary, reflecting comments Mr. Roddenberry made during our 1984 interview with him.

What I soon discovered was the lineage of ownership that *Star Trek*'s early series had gone through.

- 1965: Desilu Studios. Shown on NBC.
- 1967: Desilu bought by Gulf and Western, parent company of Paramount and renamed Paramount TV.
- 1993: Viacom buys Paramount.
- 2000: CBS becomes part of Viacom and now is tied to Paramount.
- 2006: CBS and Viacom split.
- 2018: CBS represents *Star Trek* TV rights. Paramount owns *Star Trek* feature-film rights.

Once we found out the current license owner and approached them for a clearance, we spent several weeks talking with several executives. The price for a one-minute clip would eventually be offered at $20,000. If we added the union clearances it would be about $30,000. This did not include music.

Since this was close to the working budget of the entire documentary, we painfully realized we could not afford to license this material. This changed the entire focus of the documentary.

❦ SUMMARY

Television stations and networks commissioned tens of thousands of hours of programming, dating from today back to the early 1940s. The ownership of this material is split between local stations, television networks and independent production companies. The ownership has often changed hands several times over the years.

If you need material from these sources, the challenge is going to be first figuring out who presently owns it—if anyone—and second, who actually has copies. Expect to possibly pay two separate license fees for rights and acquisition, in addition to any possible talent-clearance payments.

CHAPTER 22

SPECIAL COLLECTIONS

⚘ INTRODUCTION

You spend your life collecting one particular thing. Stamps, coins, dolls, paintings. Twenty years later, your spouse has left you and you have rooms full of your "collectibles." You finally realize you may have gone overboard.

The world is full of these "special collections." You can find them and many collectors are very happy to share their collection.

These collections have strange lives. The collectors' lives become intertwined with their goodies and often not in a particularly healthy way. At some point they die. None of their relatives loved

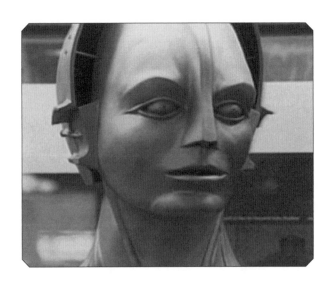

FIGURE 22.1.
Forrest Ackerman's private science fiction museum, which included the *Metropolis Woman*. Footagesource.com

FIGURE 22.2. Magic Lantern, circa 1890. Forsher Collection.

their passion and in fact have developed a severe dislike for valuables they often see as "stuff."

If the family is lucky, they have a collection of priceless art. It goes to Sotheby's and a few million dollars later, everyone is happy. Maybe this collection of "things" has some historic worth and may avoid being put into a dumpster by finding a new home. These are called "special collections." For the rest, the resourceful few figure they can get a few bucks on eBay.

Whatever the story, the objects in these collections are a huge and invaluable resource to filmmakers. The challenge is both finding them and having the patience to hear hours of stories from collectors.

✽ HOW DO YOU FIND THE COLLECTORS?

Some careful internet searches using the titles you are looking for may be a great start. You can visit large antique markets that are often held in cities throughout the year and talk with the dealers about who they suggest might have what you are looking for. Many times, state and federal archives know who they are. You can also look at copies of newspapers like *Classic Images* or *Collector's Weekly* that appeal to the collector market.

✓ AND ONCE THEY DIE?

What happens to these special collections when the collector dies? If they are worth a lot of money, the family arranges for the collectibles all to be sold off. If not, they need to find an institution to adopt the collection. Historical societies, museums and university libraries have become the destination of first choice.

Colleges and universities offer some of the best private collections. Many alumni leave their valuable papers and collectibles to their favorite school. You can find these collections through internet searches.

Each institution has different rules and fees. Some charge fees for research and access while others don't.

✓ CAN YOU USE MATERIAL IN COLLECTIONS?

This is not legal advice. As a filmmaker, my rule of thumb has been the "anybody could have shot it" rule. If you have found a generic 1940 shot of the Statue of Liberty and nobody is in the picture, you are pretty safe. A hundred people can claim shooting this shot.

If it is a home Christmas party full of strangers, each one of these people could be the call claiming you invaded their privacy and wanting money.

Evaluate each element you get as a separate annoying phone call possibility. Even if you get a great archival element from a collector, ask yourself if anyone else can put a claim on it.

❧ SUMMARY

Thousands of unique private collections exist around the world. Once the collector dies, libraries, universities and historic societies have found themselves the repositories of interesting historic collections put together by these private individuals. The biggest challenge is finding the collection; a job made much easier with the help of search engines and keywords.

When negotiating with the host institution, find out if they are willing to license the material you need. Inquire if the donation has any limitations on secondary usage. Many collections are donated with the stipulation that it is only available for research and not to be used in films, TV shows or books.

CHAPTER 23

IN YOUR COMMUNITY

🌿 INTRODUCTION

Sometimes stories and research opportunities just fall in our laps. A neighbor becomes a war hero. Your uncle created a product used by millions and sold off the rights for $100. Your place of business is destroyed by a tornado. Situations like these exist all around the country. Any of these stories and a thousand just like them often make for a captivating storyline that can be used as the basis for a powerful documentary, feature film or TV show.

FIGURE 23.1. Protestors marching against segregated movie theaters. Tallahassee, Florida, circa 1965. Footagesource.com

❧ INTERESTING PERSONALITIES

"Interesting personalities" are often great interviewees for the show you are working on. However, working with a non-professional has its own special problems. One must learn how to get along with personalities who are often times shy, abrasive or just plain challenging. If one can surmount these issues, the shows that materialize are often both enlightening and entertaining.

Some of the best documentaries come to life when they allow us into a world we can't believe is real and not fiction. Look around. They are at offices, churches, temples, schools, and often just next door. Many times these are the people that we normally avoid, but as subjects in a film, they can become both colorful and enlightening.

Be aware that many people simply do not want to be exposed to a camera and prefer to be left alone. Filmmakers often spend considerable time just getting to know their future subjects to gain a

FIGURE 23.2. Good Humor truck, circa 1956. Home movie collection. Los Angeles. Footagesource.com

level of trust and comfort to get their permission to appear in the documentary.

Programs like Terry Zwigoff's 1997 documentary *Crumb* came to life only because underground artist R. Crumb and his unusual family allowed the filmmaker to capture their true spirit.

YOUR FAMILY PAPERS AND COLLECTIONS

If your family kept a record of important events over the course of the years, you are fortunate to have a wonderful collection of research materials at your fingertips. Papers, photographs, newspapers and home movies not only document your own life, but the history of your community, the fashions of the day, the cars driven over the years and the popular culture of the last few decades. This is a great place to start finding these elements, since you don't generally have to worry about rights.

This works well for any twentieth-century–related history project, personal diary documentaries and establishing shots for investigative reports.

For those interested in doing a personal documentary, your life and your extended family's lives are full of stories. Some of these become tales that are recounted to others over the years. These are your special experiences that become landmarks in your life, events such as surviving a challenging childhood, an impossible marriage or six months of combat duty. Many of the great documentaries over the years began by the filmmaker realizing that one of these stories would lend themselves well to the screen.

COMMUNITY GROUPS

Throughout the world, nearly every community has a series of battles that are taking place as you are reading this. You can find them in the papers, leaflets and even neighborhood gossip sites. Often social action groups form when enough people in the community react to a common concern. They form associations and work together to fight. These situations can often lend themselves to fantastic fiction and non-fiction stories with tremendous dramatic results. Great interviews, a lot of smartphone-captured rallies and more.

These groups range from historical societies to political action groups and cover an entire range of our contemporary shared experience.

TAKING ADVANTAGE OF YOUR EVERYDAY ENCOUNTERS

When I started producing films in the 1970s, our world had fewer distractions. No cable TV. No cell phones. No smartphones. No computers.

How did we survive? To fill the time, people communicated by words, face to face. In so doing, we learned interesting facts about people's lives, their families and the adventures they experienced.

Yes, we can do a Google search or visit Facebook pages and learn some great facts about famous people. But to get the most out of the people in your community and the knowledge they possess, you will have to dust off the age-old art of conversation and go hunt for the great stories and resources that exist right down the block.

SUMMARY

Whether it be fiction or non-fiction films, they all share the common ingredient of a powerful story that audiences can relate to.

Well-funded Hollywood producers have the luxury of "optioning" books and articles that a writer has created reflecting a great story. For the rest of us, our world serves the same purpose. We are surrounded by stories that can make a great film.

You have a number of incredible resources readily available to you that can offer you the inspiration and material to make your next film.

ASSIGNMENT TWO

Create a research report that shows your efforts to find film clips. Take this list and under each main category write down a list of places to look for material.

You might want to create two lists under each area. The first would be affordable sources like the National Archives, your family home-movie collection or your local state film archive. Your second list will be the "for profit" sources of material like movie studios or film archive companies.

Take your time making this list. This will be your guide in moving forward. You might discover you can get everything you need from the lower-cost sources. You might also find that you are stuck with movie studios and their higher costs.

PART THREE

HOW TO LICENSE IT

CHAPTER 24

UNDERSTANDING THE LAW 101

❧ INTRODUCTION

Entertainment is a very litigious area. Hollywood may have more lawyers than any other area in the United States besides New York, the other media center. Most people who have spent years creating a project feel strongly about protecting their hard work. So do studios, who are in business for one reason: to make money. If they see one of their films being used without proper consent, they can be downright scary.

FIGURE 24.1. Three Stooges *Disorder in the Court* (1936). One of the very few Three Stooges titles that fell into the public domain. Footagesource.com

The following chapter is not "legal advice" since I am not a law-yer. It is practical advice as a producer and archivist who has had to produce and license archival material while working with the many laws in place. I encourage you to find a smart lawyer at some point and when you have an issue that you don't have a solution for, spend the money to solve the problem before it becomes a bigger one.

🌶 THE LEGAL BASICS

It goes without much saying that when you think to yourself, "Ah, I can get away with that," you already know you are making a very expensive gamble.

But it isn't hard to avoid the headaches of a lawsuit. Most producers don't find themselves in court every week. One learns that the first thing you need to know about your archival material is whether it will fit into one of these three areas:

- 🌶 Copyright
- 🌶 Public domain
- 🌶 Fair use

🌶 WHAT IS COPYRIGHT?

Ever notice a warning that looks something like this?

This DVD contains copyrighted material and the footage on it can-not be used for third-party uses. You cannot take this material and make another show and sell it without a film license agreement.

This brings us to copyright law. Copyright law in the United States is built to protect the authors of films, videos, music, and sto-ries. Copyright in a work created on or after 1976 falls into these categories:

(a) **Individual works**—Except as provided by the following subsections, the copyright endures for a term consisting of the life of the author and 70 years after the author's death.

(b) **Joint works**—In the case of a joint work prepared by two or more authors who did not work for hire, the copyright endures for a term consisting of the life of the last surviving author and 70 years after such last surviving author's death.

(c) **Anonymous works**—In the case of an anonymous work, a pseudonymous work, or a work made for hire, the copyright endures for a term of 95 years from the year of its first publication, or a term of 120 years from the year of its creation, whichever expires first.

The best place to begin looking for information about US copyright law is by going directly to the website of the US Copyright Office at https://www.copyright.gov/title17/

The Copyright Act of 1976 extended copyright for the life of the author plus 50 years, or 75 years for a work of corporate authorship. In 1998, Congress gave the studios and producers added protection with the Copyright Term Extension Act (CTEA). This extended copyright terms in the United States to life of the author plus 70 years and for works of corporate authorship to 120 years after creation or 95 years after publication, whichever ends earlier.

One criticism of copyright law is the long copyright terms. When you study the history of US copyright law, one realizes that it has evolved to its present state over nearly two centuries.

When the United States passed its first copyright act in 1790, the term was set at 14 years. In the 1920s it was 28 years with a possible renewal of 28 years. Today's copyright is nearly triple the 28-year limit and many copyright holders have been demanding that it be extended to even greater lengths of time.

A creative project produced from 1976 onward is likely going to remain in copyright for most of our lives. However, films produced before 1976 had 28-year-term copyrights that were renewable. If a film was not renewed in its 28th year, it fell into the public domain.

Having said that, remember that exemptions always exist. A copyrighted film clip may be edited into a government film. It doesn't make that clip public domain. A state may donate its holdings to a private archive that may set a license rate to access the film. Just be prepared for every type of exception possible and don't assume you are right about anything. When it comes to protecting their valuable assets, copyright holders are not your friend.

❦ WHAT IS PUBLIC DOMAIN?

The public domain means that no intellectual property rights exist. Works in the public domain may be used without any restrictions. Works can enter into the public domain in different ways.

- ❦ Copyrights expire. This means that the work was copyrighted, but when the time came to renew the copyright, the copyright holders forgot, were dead or the company that owned it just didn't exist. Either way, their loss is our gain.

- ❦ Authors put their work in the public domain before the copyright expires. Using a Public Domain Dedication, this allows anyone to waive their copyright and place a work directly into the global public domain prior to the expiration of copyright.

- ❦ They were never subject to copyright protection in the first place. Government films, facts, natural events and the like cannot be copyrighted. We pay taxes, so the thinking is that the citizens financed the film and they then own it. This includes an incredible number of films. In the United States, you will find the NASA catalog and all the government films in the National Archives. Many state-produced films also are in the public domain.

❦ HOW TO PROVE IT IS PUBLIC DOMAIN

A helpful first step is to get hold of a copy of the three-volume *Film Superlist*. This out-of-print book lists all copyrighted material from 1894 to 1959 and lists which titles have been renewed or not. This will *not* be your final legal authorization to call a film public domain, but it will give you all the information you will need on the title, registration and date of publication. Hopefully, a library near you has a copy of this. Otherwise, be prepared to spend a substantial amount to purchase a used copy.

At the end of the day, you should be able to prove that your material is in the public domain. The most efficient way to do this is to hire a Library of Congress researcher (see website below) or an independent researcher in Washington, DC, and have them do a copyright search for the titles you believe are in the public domain or copyright titles for which you might not be sure who the current owner truly is. They will issue you a report and describe when the archival element fell into the public domain or that no copyright ever was issued.

WEBSITE— https://www.copyright.gov/rrc/

⌐ *SPOTLIGHT ON* . . .

IT'S A WONDERFUL LIFE

Many motion pictures have fallen into the public domain. One of the most famous is It's a Wonderful Life. *Produced and directed by Frank Capra, it was financed by a production company called Liberty Films. The film was released in 1946 and was considered a commercial failure. Twenty-eight years after its release, Liberty Films did not exist anymore. Nobody came along to renew the copyright.*

FIGURE 24.2. *It's A Wonderful Life* (1946) movie poster.

Television stations in the United States found out that it was public domain and in the early 1970s started airing the film around the holidays. Pretty soon it found the popularity that it never achieved when first released and took on the title of being a classic.

Once film distributors saw that it was both public domain and very popular, they tried to capitalize on its fame. The film was colorized in the 1980s and this version was given a new copyright. Other distributors went back to underlying rights and acquired the music rights and then claimed they owned the black-and-white version, too. Before long, only one station in each market was showing the film.

✔ WHAT IS FAIR USE?

Fair use is a legal doctrine that promotes freedom of expression by permitting the unlicensed use of copyright-protected works in certain circumstances. The United States Copyright Office offers some basic guidance for establishing "fair use" protection for using copyrighted material.

Section 107 of the Copyright Act provides the statutory framework for determining whether something is a fair use and identifies certain types of uses—such as criticism, comment, news reporting, teaching, scholarship, and research—as examples of activities that may qualify as fair use.

If you study the various court cases that have tried to define when one can claim "fair use" and when one should not try to claim a fair-use defense for using copyright material, you will find some clear examples of when to use it (news broadcasts) and when not to use it (a commercial film meant for profit). There are dozens of cases in the "gray area" that have court decisions that range all over the place.

Again, I am not giving legal advice as much as practical advice from having made films for over four decades. For the most part, I have discovered that few people are concerned about the fair-use protection *unless* money is involved. Your project will usually not get onto a copyright-holder's radar because it didn't make commercial sales. *However*, if a film starts to make a lot of money, charges of a fair-use infraction become much more common.

The other time fair use is challenged deals with a personal issue. If someone sees a copyrighted product they own and do not like the way you used it, and they can afford a legal team, then watch out. Your life is about to be made miserable. You might win in court, but your lawyer is the real winner.

I leave you with this final word of advice about claiming fair use. You can never go wrong when you "err on the side of caution."

WEBSITE—
https://www.copyright.gov/fair-use/

❦ WHAT ARE UNDERLYING RIGHTS?

Underlying rights refer to all the different copyright elements that may be part of a creative work. These include:

- ❦ Music
- ❦ Story
- ❦ Graphics

When you secure a license to use a creative work, find out what underlying rights you will also have to secure. Sometimes they are all owned by the licensor. Sometimes they only have the rights to the creative work and you will need to secure additional rights separately.

❦ CLEARING TALENT

Don't forget about talent. This may not be a copyright issue but you will need to clear all talent for creative work produced after 1960. But if you are using them for advertising reasons, 1960 SAG rules no longer apply since you are exploiting a brand . . . the talent. If an estate exists that is protecting a famous personality no matter how many years ago they died, be prepared to pay. Just look at Elvis Presley, Marilyn Monroe or James Dean. Their estates are often making more money now than the artists did when alive.

❦ WHAT ARE THE DIFFERENCES IN RIGHTS IN THE UNITED STATES VS. ABROAD?

For most of the twentieth century, filmmakers had to deal with two separate geographic copyrights; the United States and abroad.

Most of the world had signed on to the Berne Convention copyright agreement that went back to 1886. The United States didn't want any part in it. Thus, a film could be copyrighted in Europe but fall into public domain in the United States (including such classics as Fritz Lang's *Metropolis*).

In 1989 the United States finally realized that two copyright tribunals were not in anyone's interest and ratified the Berne Convention. As of 2018, there are 175 countries around the world that are parties to the Berne Convention.

This did not solve all disagreements. Berne and the US copyright periods are not in agreement in all areas. Also, most underlying rights have to be examined one by one. For example, you need to license music in the United States to broadcast it here. However, in Europe, you need to fill out a music cue sheet and submit it to whomever licenses your show. They pay the music copyright holder a license fee.

✋ WHY WORRY ABOUT LIBEL?

Libel is a legal term in which you hurt someone's reputation. Over the past twenty years, I have taught film and video production classes. I have lost count of the number of video productions in which my students made fun of fellow classmates, parents, people in the community and anyone else that was fair game.

Outside of the classroom, you probably shouldn't do that. If you accuse someone of doing something and it hurts their reputation, you can get sued. The one exception where you have greater protection is when you use "parody" or "satire" and the law has supported this use of insult as protected by the First Amendment. That has not stopped major personalities like John Oliver and Bill Maher from being sued over libel and slander, but they have successfully fought off these suits. You may still get sued, but with a parody your chances of winning are greatly enhanced.

So, if you do plan on portraying anyone in an unflattering manner, make sure a lawyer has looked at your script as well as your backup information and then gives you the green light that they will defend you if you are sued for libel.

WHY WORRY ABOUT MALICE?

Malice refers to hurting someone's reputation with ill intent. If you are sued for libel and they can prove you purposely went after them for malicious reasons, you can get yourself into even bigger trouble if found guilty.

Another piece of advice you should listen to: when in doubt, do without. I'm just trying to save you a lot of grief.

HOW ABOUT INVADING SOMEONE'S PRIVACY?

Despite millions of hours of film and television and what seems like an invasion into everyone's private life, it may seem surprising that you actually need to get permission from people to show them in your project.

If you don't, you open yourself up for an invasion-of-privacy lawsuit. This may be a small claims action. It also may be a million dollar lawsuit.

What's the big deal? Okay, here is a scenario. You are making a film and shooting on a busy corner of New York City. Your talent is walking down the block and you are capturing everyone walking aside them.

A year later, you sell your film and it is about to open in a thousand theaters across the country. Just before it opens, you get a cease and desist letter from an attorney along with a threatened lawsuit. The problem came when one of the people in your shot was with a date *but* the date was not that person's spouse. You get it? Divorce. Loss of reputation. Getting fired from a conservative place of work. All because you had to get that shot and didn't spend the extra three hundred dollars to get some legally hired extras to walk up and down the block alongside the star of the film.

☙ DON'T FORGET ABOUT PLAGIARISM

This is pretty simple. Don't copy someone's work. That is plagiarism and if you do this and somebody can prove it, they get all your profits plus some.

☙ CAN YOU COPYRIGHT TITLES?

The rule of thumb is that you cannot copyright a title. You can go into your movie book and see titles used over and over again.

The problem you get into is not with the title, but with a term lawyers like to use: unfair competition. This means that your $10,000 film has the bad fortune of having the same title as a major studio hundred-million-dollar film. Guess who is going to contact you with a team of lawyers and shut you down?

How do you protect yourself? Once you come up with a title you are best advised to immediately try to secure it. Register your product with the Writers Guild. Buy the website name with your title and then the term "the movie" or "the TV series." Even take a picture of your script with a newspaper showing the date. This helps establish a firm claim to your title and may help you negotiate getting some money if a large company comes after you to shut you down.

✦ EXECUTING A LICENSE AGREEMENT

A million attorneys, a million ways to write a contract. You should assume that everything in your show must have proper clearances to be used in your final edit. These include additional footage, interviews, performances, music performances, music publishing, artwork and locations.

✦ SUMMARY

A few final words of non-legal but practical advice.

Don't assume! Find the key information that comes with the original archival source and double-check it. Make sure you are dealing with the rightful copyright holder.

Corroborate your information by using two or three different sources to make sure you are legally using the material you have contractually paid for. Nothing ruins your budget quicker than finding out after the fact that you bought rights you didn't need.

✦ KEEP UP WITH THE NEWS

We don't know what is in store in the future. As of the writing of this book, the Trans-Pacific Partnership is in jeopardy and if it ends, the relationship with countries agreeing on copyright principles goes with it. Pay attention to the news. Events like this could really affect you.

WEBSITE—
https://creativecommons.org/2018/01/15/copyright-term-extension-finally-done/

CHAPTER 25

WHAT NEEDS TO BE LICENSED?

🌶 INTRODUCTION

Parts One and Two focused on the variety of archival material available to you and where you might find it. Part Three describes how to legally use it. This chapter involves figuring out when you need a "license agreement."

In effect, a license agreement lays out the ground rules by which you and the archival material rights holder agree on a number of issues. These usually include:

1. Your name.
2. The rights holder's name.
3. Both your places of business.
4. The title of the archival material and possibly a short description.
5. A very specific agreement on what territories this agreement covers. This means that it is good for only the United States, only France, or maybe worldwide rights. This is all negotiable. The more territories, the more places you can sell your project (and of course the more it costs).
6. What time period is the license good for? Talk to your distributors. They may tell you that you must get a license agreement for at least five, six, or seven years because that is the length of time they will need for their contracts.

Re:
Agreement for JAMES FORSHER FILM ARCHIVES

Dear   :

The following shall constitute the agreement between
JAMES FORSHER FILM ARCHIVES. herein and you,
                          , "Producer" herein,
concerning the use of film footage from the " JAMES
FORSHER FILM ARCHIVES(SEE APPENDIX 1) ", the "Film"
herein, for use in your production tentatively titled
"   ", the "Production" herein.

1. FORSHER hereby quitclaims to Producer a nonexclusive
right to incorporate and exhibit archival footage (see
appendix 1)in the territory of THE WORLD
in ALL media, for unlimited runs. subject
to the terms and conditions of this agreement.

2. In consideration of the nonexclusive rights
provided herein, Producer promises and agrees to
remit to FORSHER a fee of $1,100.00.

2A. Producer shall notify FORSHER in writing within ten (10)
days of the total amount of footage from the Film
incorporated into the Production and shall remit
to FORSHER at that time all fees due to FORSHER hereunder.

3. The consideration specified in paragraph 2 is for
the nonexclusive right to use footage from the Film
only. Producer promises and agrees that all laboratory
costs, transportation or loss expenses incurred by
either FORSHER or Producer in connection with this
agreement shall be borne exclusively by Producer.

4. Producer and FORSHER hereby acknowledge that FORSHER
cannot exercise any control whatsoever over the particular
creative decisions made by Producer concerning the use
of the film footage licensed herein, and that the
creative integration of footage from the Films into the
Production is under Producer's sole and exclusive
control.

FIGURE 25.1. Sample license agreement, front page. Footagesource.com

5. Producer and FORSHER acknowledge that so-called
"residual payments" or like fees, however denominated, may
become due certain of the performers appearing in the film
footage by virtue of the use Producer will make thereof.
Producer hereby represents and warrants that it will pay
any such "residual payments" and obtain all necessary
union permission(s) for the usage intended. Producer
hereby agrees to obtain releases from any persons in the
footage whose faces are recognizable, for permission to
appropriate their names and likenesses, acts, plays,
poses, and appearances, in any media and for all uses
provided Producer in this agreement.

6. Producer agrees, represents, and warrants to pay any
and all fees or royalties due and payable or which become
due and payable to any guilds, unions, performing rights
societies or any other such parties by virtue of its use
of footage from the Films along with the music contained
in the soundtracks thereof as integrated into the
Production. Producer hereby warrants and agrees, regardless
of and notwithstanding anything to be contrary herein,
should any claim suits or actions be brought by any party
against FORSHER its predecessors or successors-in-interest,
for nonpayment of such fees or royalties, Producer will
defend any or all of them against such claims, suits or
actions at Producer's sole expense. Producer further
agrees that it will indemnify FORSHER, its predecessors or
successors-in-interest, and any or all of them and hold
them harmless from any judgements, attachments, losses
incurred by them because of injunction or because of
other legal and equitable relief, obtained by a third
party described in this paragraph or in paragraph five (5).

7. Should any claims, suits, judgements, attachments or
legal or equitable actions be brought by any party against
FORSHER, its predecessors or successors-in-interest, based
upon Producer's usage of footage from the Films for injury
to personal or business reputation or based upon
infringements of right to publicity, privacy, or based upon
any other rights, Producer will defend any or all of them
against such claims, suits or actions at its sole expense.
Producer further hereby warrants and agrees that regardless
of and notwithstanding anything to the contrary herein,
that Producer will indemnify FORSHER, its predecessors or
successors-in-interest and hold any or all of them harmless
from any claims, suits, judgements or attachments, and any
other relief legal or equitable.

7. Limitations of the license. The rights holder may specify what rights they have and don't have.

8. Date agreement begins and ends. This ideally means all media, worldwide in perpetuity. If they don't give you this and your distributor says that you cannot distribute your film with a limited time frame, you need to put on your negotiating hat and say something.

☙ WHAT NEEDS TO BE CLEARED

This process is the same for all creative works, including not only feature films but:

- ☙ Television programs
- ☙ Rock videos

---

8. FORSHER and Producer agree that this footage rights agreement and all questions of the rights and obligations of the parties, shall be interpreted or otherwise resolved pursuant to the laws of the State of California governing contracts negotiated, entered and to be performed therein. Further, Producer and FORSHER hereby consent to exclusively resolve or litigate any disputes which may arise between Producer and FORSHER concerning our mutual and several rights and obligations under this agreement only in the state courts of California.

9. It is hereby understood and agreed that this letter of agreement constitutes the complete, final and entire understanding as between the parties, and no amendment, supplement, modification of this agreement shall be binding unless the same is in writing and executed by the duly authorized officers of the respective parties to this agreement.

Your signature as indicated hereinbelow shall constitute your understanding and agreement to the terms set forth hereinabove.

Very truly yours,

JAMES FORSHER FILM ARCHIVES

By:_____
　　　JAMES FORSHER

Accepted and Agreed to:

By:_____
　　NAME　　　　　TITLE

APPENDIX 1: FOOTAGE LICENSED:*
1) DANCING DEVIL (CIRC. 1905)
2) CLOCK, FAST MOTION (CIRC. 1940)
3) SPORTS EVENT (CIRC. 1962, NEWSREEL)
4) ANIMALS (CIRC. 1930)
5) DANCING WOMAN (CIRC. 1947)
6) DOLLS (CIRC. 1937)

*each clip is less than 10 seconds in length.

- Cartoons
- News programs
- Corporate films
- Educational films
- Home movies
- Film trailers
- YouTube clips

You might be shocked at how many license agreements you might end up having to secure for one archival element. Let's create a scenario in which you will need to get a license agreement for using a one-minute–long film clip from James Cameron's film *Avatar*.

First you must get the studio's permission. They will probably tell you that you also need Mr. Cameron's approval.

Once you get these agreements and negotiate a price, you have your first license agreement. Now you need to get all the underlying rights taken care of. These include:

ACTORS: Every actor appearing in the scene you want must approve the deal and agree to a payment. This will be minimally a SAG/AFTRA day-rate payment or possibly a higher rate if the actor in the clip is very prominent. The fee might also have to cover an additional ten percent for the actor's representative to make the deal.

DGA: Standard day-rate payment for the director.

WGA: Standard payment for the writer.

MUSIC LICENSE: You will need to contact the company representing the rights holder for the music in *Avatar*. They will want to know the scene and musical composition and will then quote you a fee.

You might need to pay all the musicians that played music in that scene. It depends where the music was recorded. If it was in Bulgaria, you are lucky and probably not liable for this payment. If the music is performed by musicians who are members of the American Federation of Musicians (AFM), the federation will dictate the fee for use of these musicians' music.

GRAPHICS: If any copyrighted images are in the scene, they must be licensed from the artist or their representative.

You may have some additional clearances. These include dealing with estates representing talent that is deceased and producers that still hold onto some rights.

❧ HOW DO YOU "CLEAR" RIGHTS?

This is not for the faint of heart. The first step as mentioned before is to go through the research process and find the current rights holder. These will often be large companies with many departments.

It may take several phone calls or internet searches to find the department handling your particular type of rights clearance. I suggest you initially write the appropriate person, explain what your project is about and the rights you will need. Follow this up with a phone call within the week. If you are lucky, you can begin the negotiation.

As I have mentioned in the past chapters, if you have the money in your budget, hiring an expert "clip clearance" person makes a lot of sense. They will cost between a few hundred and a few thousand dollars—depending on how complicated the job is—but you are buying years of experience and contacts throughout the industry that you can only dream of having. They know a good price and they know when you are being robbed and will tell you since they work for you.

⌒ *SPOTLIGHT ON . . .*

Clip Clearance Expert JAMES TUMMINIA

❧ How would you describe your job?

My job as a clearance consultant is to help facilitate and support a filmmaker's vision and the story to be told, creatively and budgetarily. I discuss the audio/visual assets the filmmaker wants to include and provide a general idea of what the costs would be. With that wish list and a sense of the budget, I approach licensors directly to negotiate the terms of the license, including rights required and licensing fees, and in some cases, supervise the process to secure permission or consent (from an actor, a studio) based on the asset's use in the project. If cost or permission issues arise, we work together to find a creative and budgetary balance while not sacrificing story. My job also involves maintaining relationships with licensors, knowing how their assets inventory is evolving and how their assets can be integral parts of stories.

❧ What should producers and editors do to prepare before contacting you?

Producers and editors should have as clear a vision as possible of what assets are to be targeted, how much of the project will use licensed material, the budget for licensing and clearances services, and a realistic and reasonable schedule to get it done, including, but not limited to, research and getting quotes, negotiating terms, reviewing licenses and receiving master material.

❧ What are common mistakes you see when working with researchers and producers?

The common mistakes researchers and producers make primarily have to do with being realistic about marketplace licensing fees and terms, and scheduling. Many don't realize the costs of getting "grand rights" (all media, worldwide, in perpetuity) can be astronomically high and easily break a tight budget. Generally, I recommend licensing what rights are contractually needed (if grand rights aren't) and consider negotiating options for rights that may be needed later based on the budget.

There are certain terms that can adversely impact an editor's creative style, too. Often, licensors charge a per-minute fee or have a minimum (e.g., 30 seconds). Many quick cuts from many sources would mean paying a lot more for a lot less than is being used. The time it takes to get content licensed can vary and producers and editors must factor that in.

This includes bringing a clearance professional on board as early as possible for a project that is heavy in licensable material so there is enough time to get quotes, negotiate terms, review and get mutually approved licenses, and order master material.

It may sound cliché, but the devil is in the detail. Don't leave sourcing until the end; start the process right now. The internet is a great place to find audio/visual assets, but the copyright owner might not have or probably has not posted the asset. Finding who has the copyright could be time consuming.

JAMES TUMMINIA
Clearances Consultant/Producer
jamestumminia@yahoo.com

☙ SUMMARY

For all archival material that is not in the public domain, you must secure a license agreement. These agreements come in many forms but the basic information as spelled out earlier in the chapter protects both you and the rights holder, clarifying the legal use of their product in your production.

Finally, think carefully about what you ask for with the future in mind. Not just what you need today, but try to clear what you will

BISON
"101"
BISON ARCHIVES
Marc Wanamaker
1600 Schuyler Road
Beverly Hills, CA 90210
(213) 276-9491 /
– Motion Picture History –
©1912 NEW YORK MOTION PICTURE CO. INC.

December 15, 1983

JAMES FORSHER PRODUCTIONS
BEST SHOW IN TOWN PRODUCTIONS
650 N. Bronson Ave.
Hollywood Calif. 90004

TICKET TO HOLLYWOOD: Still photographs and poster clearances

PUBLICITY SHOTS ARE GENERALLY BEHIND THE SCENE SHOTS AND ARE NOT COPYRIGHTED. THEY ARE PUBLIC DOMAIN SHOTS.

1. POSTER: "Stand-In" / License agreement secured with Stan Caidin
2. STILL: 'Hollywoodland' sign   1926 / Public Domain
3. POSTER: Wm. S. Hart (Only face is shown) / Public Domain
4. POSTER: Charles Chaplin (Only face is shown) / Public Domain
5. POSTER: Roscoe Arbuckle (Only face is shown) /Public Domain
6. STILL: Laurel and Hardy with Hal Roach (in front of offices).
             (This shot is a publicity shot, not copyrighted)
7. STILL: OUR GANG   (Behind the scene shot-not copyrighted)
8. POSTER: OUR GANG   (Sections of the poster are used)/Public Domain
9. STILL: MASCOT STUDIO--Aerial 1934 (The Mascot studios are
             defunct and their films on the most part are public domain.
             Exterior shots of studios are also, Public Domain.)
10. STILL: Paramount Casting Call 1930 / (Behind the scenes shot
                                                    public Domain)
11. STILL: Paramount Train w/Extra Girls 1936 / (Publicity shot
                                                    public Domain)
12. STILL: Paramount Casting Call 1936 / (Publicity shot-Public Domain)
13. STILL: Publicity Parade 'Souls for Sale' float 1920's
                                                    (Publicity Shot-Public Domain)
14. STILL: Hallum Cooley (actor) (Publicity shot-Public domain, no
                                                    copyright)
15. STILL: Paramount studio, 'Gentlemen prefer Blondes'
                    Gate shot. (Publicity Shot-Public Domain)
16. POSTER: THE EMPEROR JONES with Paul Robson (Public Domain film)
17. STILL: Roscoe Arbuckle in a scene from a Keystone film.
                    (Keystone films are public domain)
18. STILL: Roscoe Arbuckle from 'Gasoline Gus' (Portrait shot-publicity)
                                                    (Publicity shot-public domain)
19. STILL: Roscoe Arbuckle Trial (Newspaper shot-defunct newspaper)
20. STILL: "   "   "   "   "   "   "
21. STILL: William Desmond Taylor Portrait (Publicity shot-Public domain)
22. STILL: Mabel Normand Portrait (Publicity shot-Public Domain)
23. STILL: Wallace Reid and wife 1920 (Publicity shot-Public Domain)
24. STILL: Jackie Cooper with camera (Publicity shot-public domain)
25. STILL: Jackie Cooper at doorway 1932 (Publicity shot-public domain)
26. STILL: Shirley Temple in director's

FIGURE 25.2. Sample license agreement for archival footage.

– ESTABLISHED 1909 –

BISON ARCHIVES
Marc Wanamaker
1600 Schuyler Road
Beverly Hills, CA 90210

– Motion Picture History –
(213) 276-9491

TRADE MARK

NEW YORK MOTION PICTURE CO.

MANUFACTURERS OF
'BISON LIFE MOTION PICTURES'

December 15, 1983

JAMES FORSHER PRODUCTIONS
BEST SHOW IN TOWN PRODS.
650 N. BRONSON AVE
HOLLYWOOD CALIF. 90004

Attached is a list of visuals used in the production,
TICKET TO HOLLYWOOD. The photographs and posters used in the
film are on the most part PUBLIC DOMAIN.

The ownership of the above mentioned visuals are on the most part
have lapsed over the years. The photographs that are 'behind the
scenes' or 'publicity shots' were never copyrighted, and were used
for magazine and newspaper purposes. When one uses scenes from
films (Still photographs), then usually they were under some sort of
copyright and have to be cleared. But in the case of TICKET TO
HOLLYWOOD, that is NOT the concern.

The sources of gathering the stills and posters are from THE
BISON ARCHIVES. The Bison Archives is a photographic Archives
relating directly to the history of the Motion Picture Industry
and the 'behind the scenes' in the Industry.

The visuals from the BISON ARCHIVES are all publicity-behind the scene
material and is cleared as PUBLIC DOMAIN.

The BISON ARCHIVES has supplied visual material for over 40 books and
hundreds of periodicals relating to this field.

need in a year, five or even ten years. Many producers had not heard of the technology of streaming in 1995. In fact, with download rates of two to three minutes for a simple picture, it was not a technology anyone worried about.

However, there were a few smart lawyers even back then that said they should include this delivery mechanism in license agreements. Ten years later, those lawyers were telling their clients how lucky they were to have such a sharp attorney working for them. They saved them thousands of dollars in revised license agreements fees.

So pay attention to the various emerging technologies and include these in your plans when feasible. This means 3-D, virtual reality and whatever else comes our way over the next few years.

Over the years I used several versions of this film license agreement (see Figure 25.2).Some were as short as a page while others where several pages long. They all shared the basic language that makes an agreement between the archive and producer, the time period of the agreement and the geography covered by the license.

LICENSE FEE SCHEDULE—FEBRUARY 4, 1987

RESEARCH	$45.00 per hour	1 hour min.
WINDOW DUBS	$20.00 basic +	$10.00 per min.

MEDIA:	PER MINUTE	PER SECOND
Theatrical Distribution	$1,200.00	$20.00
Include nationwide television broadcast and pay/cable transmission:	$1,350.00	$22.50
• • • •		
Television broadcast and pay/cable transmission:		
Local	$500.00	$15.00
Nationwide (network or syndication)	$900.00	$30.00
• • • •		
Television broadcast on non-commercial (PBS) stations only:		
Local	$500.00	$15.00
Nationwide	$600.00	$20.00
• • • •		
Pay/Cable television transmission only:		
Local	$500.00	$15.00
Nationwide	$750.00	$25.00
• • • •		
Home videocassette sales/rentals in addition to any of the above Media, add	$300.00	$5.00
Educational, non-commercial distribution in addition to any of the above Media, add	$150.00	$2.50
• • • •		
Home videocassette sales/rentals only	$750.00	$12.50
• • • •		
Educational, non-commercial distribution only (non-broadcast):		
Local	$600.00	$10.00
Nationwide	$900.00	$15.00
World-wide	$1,200.00	$20.00
• • • •		
Television commercials:		
Local (one market)	$500.00	$15.00
Nation-wide	$650.00	$22.50
• • • •		
Corporate presentations, live events, concerts, etc.:		
Local (one station)	$500.00	$15.00
Nationwide	$600.00	$20.00
• • • •		

The following discounts apply to all the aforementioned license fees:
    20% off the total license fee if 3 mins. of footage or more is used.
    30% off the total license fee if 5 mins. of footage or more is used.
    50% off the total license fee if 10 mins. of footage or more is used.
The fees listed in this schedule are subject to change without notice. Additional charges may apply for special handling. For further information, call:
    Michael Yakaitis, Director of Research and Sales (213) 461-0178

CHAPTER 26

NEGOTIATING ARCHIVAL MATERIAL

☙ INTRODUCTION

You have arrived at the beginning of the end. After a determined search for materials you have located the contact for the person or company that owns the rights. Now comes the fun part. You must negotiate the rights for the archival material you need at a price you can afford.

FIGURE 26.1. 1950s negotiation. From *Free Enterprise at Work*. Footagesource.com

❧ NEGOTIATING 101

Remember that you can and should negotiate. There is nothing wrong with getting the archival material owner's first price and saying that your budget will only allow for you to pay a smaller price. If they won't budge, they won't budge. Try listening to them. They will tell you in words and tone of voice what is going on. You might hear that you are lucky just to get a license and if you say another word, that will be rescinded. You might get the "I would help but I am not in the position to change our standard price." Then again, your bargaining may help. The rest of the chapter explains some tools you can use to get the best price.

❧ MATH, MARKETS & MEDIA

You get a license that defines three important elements: the "territory" that the license will cover, the type of "media" you need and the "time period" you will need.

This is where the math comes in. The more footage or archival material you want, the less the archive will charge you per item. That means, if you can get most of your material from one source, you will be able to negotiate a better overall deal since the archive will be making some decent money. The other thing to keep in mind is that less may not mean more—meaning that getting the absolute minimum amount of material may not save you as much as you think and will hurt the quality of your program.

❧ PRICING BY "TERRITORIES"

The first word to know is "territory." All media is broken into regions of the world, known as territories. A very successful film will sell in all the major territories including Europe, Southeast Asia, North America, etc.

Not all films are meant to be shown globally. Do some research by talking with distributors early on and finding out where they realistically can sell your program. Once you know where you are going to sell this project, you can then ask for those rights only.

Typically you will ask for the following territories, depending on the project's potential sales.

Local: Least expensive, this covers a city or state.

Domestic: This gives you the right for an entire country.

Worldwide & Beyond: This includes all territories on the planet Earth. Many contracts nowadays also go into the cosmic realm and include language that implies "All Media" and "All Territories" outside of our planet, too. Strange, but you never know where movies or television shows are going to be seen in twenty or thirty years.

✿ PRICING BY MEDIA MARKETS

Each territory has different types of media markets. Media markets refer to the different technologies that bring programming to the audience. They are very different in their licensing fee structures. The licensor generally knows who pays the most and who pays the least, and charges accordingly. These media markets include:

Networks: These include domestic over-the-air television airing. Budgets are typically large, and the license fee will be top dollar.

National Pay Cable: Companies like HBO and Showtime also reach millions of people and national cable channels give producers a substantial amount to cover production costs. The license fee will be close to the TV network's fee.

Basic Cable: Companies like Discovery and Arts & Entertainment offer their producers substantially less money, but offer their producers episodic programs. Producers and licensors can strike a deal in which the producer promises to buy a large number of archival elements if the licensor reduces the per-asset fee.

Local Independent TV and PBS: Local shows have very limited budgets. You might be able to negotiate a reduced cost if you are involved in a series, but even the reduced fee may not be worth the licensor's time and they may tell you as much.

Non-Broadcast: These are shows produced for corporate or educational use and have a limited audience. They will typically have the lowest rate of any archival asset.

Home Video: Twenty-five years ago, licensing for home video cost the same as for pay cable. Nowadays it is often thrown into the license agreement since so few DVD copies are sold. Having said that, certain titles that might still sell hundreds or thousands of DVDs and downloads will not go unnoticed by the licensor and you might be charged a higher fee.

Internet: With the relatively recent successes of internet-based networks like Netflix, Hulu, Apple and Amazon, licensors have found a lucrative new market. Be prepared to pay the same as cable channels, depending on which system you make a sale to.

✽ TIME PERIOD

Licensors have been all over the map when it comes to license time periods. In the past, they would prefer to limit the time period, hoping you will come back, and have been reticent to give lifetime licenses, with many clever rights holders only giving three to five years. The problem with that is that many sales will require up to seven years. If that is the case, the sale will fail or you might have to go back and redo the license.

This is where your homework comes in handy. Find out what most distributors you might use expect in terms of license time periods. Currently, the most common licensing term is *all media, worldwide, in perpetuity*. Licensors are not partial to breaking out licenses for specific terms and territories. They know they cannot monitor broadcasts in one hundred countries.

✐ WHEN TO BARGAIN AND WHEN TO COUNT YOURSELF LUCKY

After you agree on the territories, media and time period, you will have your chance to possibly bring the price down. Rights holders expect this and can be quite unpleasant.

I recently co-produced a television show with a filmmaker not used to working with American archives. We had found a substantial amount of great footage that he had fallen in love with. I had warned him about the possible costs that were beyond his budget, but he was determined to make the best film possible and ignored my advice.

When we had locked the film, I contacted the archival house that had given us the most footage and gave them the total number of clips and minutes. They came back with a price of around $30,000. My co-producer naturally hit the roof and blamed me for getting him in this situation. He then told me to call the archival house and tell them that we would scrub the entire project if they didn't substantially reduce the price.

While I was communicating this message, I realized as a former owner of a film archive that this was probably the third producer that day to make the same threat. We went back and forth and I was able to bring the price down a bit but still give the rights holder a decent check.

Not an easy way to make a living.

HOW YOU CAN SHOOT YOURSELF IN THE FOOT

If you have a dollar figure in mind, two things might happen. You stick to it and get it or you might end up with nothing. The reason is that the price you think an archival asset is worth may have no corresponding sense of reality with the market price for footage. You will then upset the person you have been working with who will not return your phone calls. Now what?

This is when you remembered my advice from a few pages back about having a clip clearance person negotiating for you. You should still know everything we are discussing in this book. This will help you communicate and get the right material through using a clip clearance person. But you do not have years of established relationships nor well-honed schmoozing skills that most clip clearance people bring to their job and this will cost you. The clip clearance person will hopefully fix the mess you are in and negotiate a fee that works for both you and the licensor.

SPOTLIGHT ON . . .

USING A CLIP CLEARANCE PROFESSIONAL

LISA KANE (1953–2018) was a clearance professional in Hollywood for many years. She worked on almost every type of television show, documentary and feature film project. Here is advice she gave for anyone planning to use a clearance professional in helping find and negotiate archival material.

What a producer and editor must have when hiring a clearance professional:

- 🌿 *Specific records of where the video came from.*
- 🌿 *The amount of footage they want to use in the project.*
- 🌿 *An awareness that the footage may be associated with guilds or unions that could drive up the costs to use the footage. Unions associated with the payment of professional actors that appear in the video, SAG/AFTRA, Writers Guild (WGA), Directors Guild (DGA), all would receive costly fees, including a high percentage pension and welfare payment for use of their footage.*
- 🌿 *The amount of money they have available for license fees.*
- 🌿 *Knowing the term and territory in which they want to distribute their project.*
- 🌿 *Knowing the amount of time they have in the schedule to get the clearances completed.*
- 🌿 *An attorney, or legal person/team to make ultimate decisions on whether they can move forward with a particular piece of footage—for example, a fair use situation.*

LISA KANE
Film Clip Clearance Professional

🌿 LEGAL REMINDERS

WHAT THE EDITOR CAN AND CAN'T DO WITH ARCHIVAL MATERIAL

Somebody needs to communicate with the producer, director and editor to make sure they are all on the same page. Editors may put footage, music or still images into a show that you discovered were cost-prohibitive. This is very important to avoid! From the beginning you should have a strong relationship with the editor. That person has to know that they have to check in with you about any element they want to add.

What you are trying to avoid is a conflict with your ultimate client, the person that will give you money for your project. The client sees the cut and naturally expects that the material in that cut will end up in the finished show. If they see a cut and then you realize you can't afford several minutes of material, your client will be angry and not understand your excuses.

What are you going to do?

MINIMUM USAGE AGREEMENTS, AND HOW THEY CAN ADD UP SUBSTANTIAL COSTS IN THE EDIT BAY

Some license agreements throw in this clause: "one minute minimum."

This seems harmless, but the problem is that your show may only use ten seconds from that clip. You are still stuck paying for a minute. If this happens four or five times in the finished program, the cost can easily be in the many thousands of dollars extra.

Try to make sure that you don't get stuck with a minute minimum. Ten seconds minimum per cut is not unusual and still guarantees the rights holder decent money on a national sale.

☙ SUMMARY

Negotiating the rights to use archival assets is an incredibly important part of the producing process. You will learn that, until you have actually negotiated terms that you can afford, never fall in love with a shot. You might be priced out of licensing it.

Negotiating rights is not set in stone. I suggest always trying to do a "step deal" in which you pay for the least costly right to secure the contract, with "steps" toward more payments once larger sales are achieved. This allows you to finish your project but not get stuck with horrendous licensing fees until decent sales come into place.

A couple of important facts to keep in mind. Most producers at this point have spent a lot of money on their shows. When I ran my own film archives, I lost count of the number of producers who complained bitterly about how broke they were and really couldn't afford archival material. I also tried to not be worried about other people's productions and stick to charging the appropriate price that allowed me to stay in business.

CHAPTER 27

ERRORS & OMISSIONS INSURANCE

✿ INTRODUCTION

You have worked hard to find the material you need for your creative project. When you found it, you negotiated a license to use it or proof that it is in the public domain. Some of you may have wondered why you have gone through such time-consuming efforts to spend a lot of money for an old film, radio program or TV show.

In short, because you and your show's buyers can be sued and you really prefer to avoid that.

And despite all your efforts proving the archival element is in the public domain or never has been copyrighted, you might still be threatened with a lawsuit anyway. This is when you wish you had taken my advice and bought an Errors & Omissions policy.

✿ PRODUCER ERRORS & OMISSIONS INSURANCE

Insurance for Errors & Omissions (E&O) is a prerequisite for qualifying for a distribution agreement for your production. Errors & Omissions insurance is not limited just to movie productions. It covers radio and television productions as well.

Nowadays a film or television program can be sold not only in the United States, but globally to nearly 200 countries. That is how distribution works. Territory by territory, they sell your program and if you are lucky, they may even pay your profit percentage.

∴nsurance Companies Los Angeles, Calif. 90010	**PRODUCERS' LIABILITY INSURANCE** **SCHEDULE AND APPLICATION** (This is an application for what is known as a "Claims Made" Policy) All Questions Must Be Answered

1. Name of Applicant: ⸱⸱ ⸱ Television Inc. & James M. Forsher Productions

2. Address: ⸱ ⸱ ⸱ , Suite 900, Los Angeles, CA 90069

  ⸱ ⸱ ⸱ Inc. is a coporation and James M. Forsher Productions is an individua
3. Is Applicant a corporation? ☒ Yes ☐ No Partnership? ☐ Yes ☐ No Individual? ☒ Yes ☐ No

4. Names and titles of principal officers, partne.⸱ ⸱ ⸱ɔans: ⸱ ⸱ ⸱ ⸱ ,
  ⸱ ⸱ ⸱ ⸱ ⸱ ; James M. Forsher, Presiden⸱

5. Desired Effective Date: February 1984 _____ Desired Term of Policy ___3___ years.

6. Limits of Desired Coverage: For any one claim: $ 1,000,000
  In the aggregate: $ 3,000,000
  Deductible amount: $ 5,000

7. Title of production to be insured: " Ticket To Hollywood ⸱ "

8. Production is: ☐ Motion Picture for initial theatrical release. Running Time: _____
  ☐ Motion Picture for initial television release. Program Time: _____
  ☐ TV Pilot ☒ TV Special ☐ Radio Program. Program Time: _73 Minutes_
  ☐ TV Series Number of Episodes: _____ Program Time: _____
  ☐ Radio Series Number each week: ___ Number of Weeks: ___ Program Time: _____
  ☐ Theatrical Presentation.

9. Has a Title Report been obtained from any one of the title clearance services? ☐ Yes ☒ No, it is pending
  If yes, name the clearance service: _____ Attach copy of Report.

10. Name, address and telephone number of Applicant's attorney: (If a firm also name individual)_____
  Xevin ⸱ ⸱ ⸱ , ⸱ ⸱ ⸱ ⸱ ⸱ ⸱ ⸱ ⸱ ⸱ ⸱ ⸱ ⸱ ⸱ ⸱ CA 90202 213-203-2225
  Bill [⸱ ⸱ ⸱], Esq., 2000 Sunset ⸱ ⸱ ⸱ , Suite 900 ⸱ ⸱ Telephone No. 21-203-2225
  Los Angeles, CA 90069
11. Has Applicant's attorney read the "Clearance Procedures" included within this Application?
  ☒ Yes ☐ No If no, explain: _____

12. Has Applicant's attorney approved as adequate the steps taken for clearance procedures used in connection with the production? ☒ Yes ☐ No
  If no, explain _____

13. Name of Producer (individual): _James M. Forsher_ Executive Producer (individual): _____

14. Names of authors and writers (including underlying works, screenplays, etc.): _James M. Forsher_

15. Will any film clips be used in this production? ☒ Yes ☐ No
  If yes, have all necessary licenses and consents been obtained? ☒ Yes ☐ No
  If no, explain: _____

-1-

FIGURE 27.1. Application for Errors & Omissions insurance. Forsher Productions.

16. Is the name or likeness of any living person used or is any living person portrayed (with or without use of name or likeness) in the production? ☒ Yes ☐ No   If so, have clearances been obtained in all cases? ☒ Yes ☐ No
(with the exception of individuals in Public Domain footage)
Is the name or likeness of any deceased person used or is any deceased person portrayed (with or without name or likeness) in the production? ☒ Yes ☐ No   If so, have clearances been obtained in all cases from personal representatives, heirs or other owners of such rights? ☒ Yes ☐ No (with the exception of individuals in Public Domain footage)

17. Are actual events portrayed in the production? ☒ Yes ☐ No

18. Has Applicant or any of its agents bargained for (a) any rights in literary, musical or other material; or (b) releases from any persons in connection with the above production, and been unable to obtain or refused an agreement or release? ☐ Yes ☒ No   If yes, explain:_____

19. Is the production: ☐ Entirely fictional.   ☒ Based on actual facts or happenings.
☐ Based on another work.   If so please specify:_____
☐ Other:_____

20. Is the production: ☐ Quiz or Panel. ☐ Interview or Forum. ☐ Variety.
☐ Musical. ☐ Dramatic. ☐ Children's Show. ☒ Documentary. ☐ Docudrama. ☐ Other._____

21. Brief resumé of production: __The history of the great Hollywood studios and stars is told__
__from the turn of the century through the thirties.__

22. Have musical rights been cleared? ☒ Yes ☐ No
(a) Recording and Synchronization rights? ☒ Yes ☐ No   (b) Performing Rights? ☒ Yes ☐ No

23. Has Applicant had prior Producers' Liability Insurance on production to be insured?
☐ Yes ☒ No   If yes, attach a copy of prior policy.

24. Has Applicant or any officers, directors or partners, ever been refused similar insurance for this production or any other production? ☐ Yes ☒ No   If yes, explain:_____

25. Applicant represents and warrants that neither it, nor any of its officers, directors or partners, or their counsel, have no knowledge, actual or constructive:
(a) of any claims or legal proceedings made or commenced against the Applicant, or any officers, directors, partners, or subsidiary or affiliated corporations within the last three (3) years for invasion of privacy, infringement of copyright (statutory or common law), defamation, unauthorized use of titles, formats, ideas, characters, plots or other program material embodied in this or any other production, or breach of implied contract arising out of alleged submission of any literary or musical material. ☒ No exceptions ☐ Except as follows: _____

(b) of any threatened claims or legal proceedings against the Applicant or any officers, directors, subsidiaries or partners or against any other person, firm or corporation arising out of or based upon the production including title thereof, or any material upon which the production is or will be based, that would be covered by the policy sought to be obtained by the Applicant. ☒ No exceptions ☐ Except as follows:_____

(c) of any facts, circumstances or prior negotiations by reason of which they, or any of them, believe that a claim might reasonably be asserted or legal proceedings instituted against the Applicant that would be covered by the policy sought to be obtained by the Applicant. ☒ No exceptions ☐ Except as follows:_____

26. Applicant agrees to use its best efforts to obtain from third parties from whom it obtains material for the production written indemnities against claims arising out of the use of such material. Initials of Applicant _____

-2-

27. Applicant agrees that it will use due diligence to determine whether any matter or materials to be used in the production are protected by law and, where necessary, to obtain from parties owning rights therein the right to use the same in connection with the production. Initials of Applicant _____

THIS APPLICATION IS SUBMITTED WITH THE FOLLOWING SPECIFIC UNDERSTANDING:

(a) Applicant warrants and represents that the above answers and statements are in all respects true and material to the issuance of an insurance policy and that Applicant has not omitted, suppressed or misstated any facts.
(b) If a policy issues hereafter, this Application shall be attached to and become a part of such policy.
(c) The signing and filing of this Application does not bind the Applicant or the Company and no insurance shall be deemed effective unless and until a written binder or policy of insurance is issued by the Company in response hereto.
(d) All exclusions in the policy apply regardless of any answers or statements in this Application.
(e) Applicant understands that the limit of liability and deductible under any policy to be issued in response hereto shall include both loss payment and claim expenses as defined in the policy.

Date: _____3/2/84_____   Applicant: Atlantic Television Inc.
                                                   James M. Forsher Productions
                                        By:_____

                                        Title: Vice President, Program Operations

Agent/Broker _____

Address _____

Telephone Number _____

CLEARANCE PROCEDURES

The following is a guide — not a complete checklist — for the Applicant's attorney who should make certain that the undernoted points have been complied with prior to final cut or first exhibition of the production to be insured:

1. The script should be read **prior** to commencement of production to eliminate matter which is defamatory, invades privacy or is otherwise potentially actionable.

2. Unless the work is an unpublished original not based on any other work, a copyright report must be obtained. Both domestic and foreign copyrights and renewal rights should be checked. If a completed film is being acquired a similar review should be made on copyright and renewals on any copyrighted underlying property.

3. If the script is an unpublished original, the origins of the work should be ascertained — basic idea, sequence of events and characters. It should be ascertained if submissions of any similar properties have been received by the applicant and, if so, the circumstances as to why the submitting party may not claim theft or infringement should be described in detail.

4. Prior to final title selection, a title report should be obtained.

(See Over)

-3-

208 ⌒

5. Whether production is fictional (and location is identifiable) or factual, it should be made certain that no names, faces or likenesses of any recognizable living persons are used unless written releases have been obtained. Release is unnecessary if person is part of a crowd scene or shown in a fleeting background. Telephone books or other sources should be checked when necessary. Releases can only be dispensed with if the applicant provides the insurer with specific reasons, in writing, as to why such releases are unnecessary and such reasons are accepted by the insurer. The term "living persons" includes thinly disguised versions of living persons or living persons who are readily identifiable because of identity of other characters or because of the factual, historical or geographic setting.

6. Releases from living persons should contain language which gives the applicant the right to edit, delete material, juxtapose any part of the film with any other film, change the sequence of events or of any questions posed and/or answers, fictionalize persons or events including the releasee and to make any other changes in the film that the applicant deems appropriate. If a minor, consent has to be legally binding.

7. If music is used, the applicant must obtain all necessary synchronization **and** performance licenses.

8. Written agreements must exist between the applicant and all creators, authors, writers, performers and any other persons providing material (including quotations from copyrighted works) or on-screen services.

9. If distinctive locations, buildings, businesses, personal property or products are filmed, written releases should be secured. This is not necessary if non-distinctive background use is made of real property.

10. If the production involves actual events it should be ascertained that the author's sources are independent and primary (contemporaneous newspaper reports, court transcripts, interviews with witnesses, etc.) and not secondary (another author's copyrighted work, autobiographies, copyrighted magazine articles, etc.).

11. Shooting script and rough cuts should be checked, if possible, to assure compliance of all of the above. During photography persons may be photographed on location, dialogue added or other matter included which was not originally contemplated.

12. If the intent is to use the production to be insured on video discs, tape cassettes or other new technology, rights to manufacture, distribute and release the production should be obtained, including the above rights, from all writers, directors, actors, musicians, composers and others necessary therefor.

13. Film clips are dangerous unless clearances for the second use are obtained from those rendering services or supplying material. Special attention should be paid to music rights, as publishers are taking the position that a new synchronization and performance license is required.

14. Aside from living persons, even dead persons (through their personal representatives or heirs) have a "right of publicity", especially where there is considerable fictionalization. Clearances should be obtained where necessary.

-4-

What Errors & Omissions insurance does is indemnify producers and their distributors from lawsuits that may arise from the content of a production, including lawsuits alleging:

- Infringement of copyright
- Libel or slander
- Invasion of privacy
- Plagiarism or unauthorized copying of ideas
- Defamation or degrading of products, otherwise known as trade libel
- Infringement on a title, a slogan, or a trademark

Any type of production may be eligible for Errors & Omissions insurance. However, Errors & Omissions must be obtained *before* the fact of distribution, not after the fact. Productions that have had prior losses due to content errors are not eligible for coverage.

⌒ SPOTLIGHT ON . . .

MY PERSONAL EXPERIENCE WITH A THREATENED LAWSUIT

Many years ago I produced an hour special for the Discovery Channel. This was when they were one channel and had limited budgets for new productions. That meant I had to cut costs and I decided that if I was going to get a producer's fee, I was not going to take out an Errors & Omissions policy.

I finished the show and completed a review of every film clip I had used, making sure I had a Library of Congress clearance report. This was not my first show and I knew exactly what to do to protect myself. I did everything I would have done for the E&O policy except pay for the cost of it.

The show aired for the three years of the agreed-upon license period with Discovery. At the final month I got a call. It's the call you dread getting, from a representative of a large production company located in Asia. They claimed that I used a clip of one of their films in my show and they wanted to be compensated with damages.

I sent them my Library of Congress report showing the film did not show ever being copyrighted in the United States. They continued to claim that they owned it and demanded money. They even had the trade mission from their country call me and threaten me.

After six months of "negotiations," I told the company representative that he should stop calling me and that he could not get blood out of a turnip. (I was truly broke at the time and was not lying.) I then politely hung up.

I assume someone explained the idiom to him and they luckily stopped bothering me.

If I had spent the additional couple of thousand dollars, I could have simply given the representative of the Asian production company the name of the attorney for the E&O insurer who was expert at negotiating these issues and I would have saved myself countless sleepless nights.

❧ HOW TO PREPARE AN E&O POLICY APPLICATION

Here are the basic steps you will have to go through to prepare an E&O application. I suggest you create a notebook that has the following items that you will need to provide the insurance company.

1. Completed final script for the program.
2. A spreadsheet of archival elements and where they fall within your program. Include columns for:
   a) Title of the archival element
   b) Owner or public domain

      c) Copy of the original document showing you have legal rights to the archival material, with a corresponding number or alphabetical link that can be found in your spreadsheet.

      d) Length used in the program

3. All license agreements as well as document releases for talent, music, director and any other underlying rights you had negotiated.

4. Contact two or three insurance companies, inquiring about receiving a quote for an E&O Policy. They will request you fill out an application.

5. Make sure you have plenty of money in the bank.

☙ SUMMARY

If your program is going to be distributed, there is a good chance the distributor and stations airing your show will request proof that you are covered by an active E&O policy. This will insure that you and the buyers do not get stuck with nuisance lawsuits that will stop the airing of the show and take all of your money.

The insurance company will make sure that *every element of the show* has a legal release or license agreement. This is where all of your hard work will pay off.

☙ LINKS TO COMPANIES OFFERING ERROR & OMISSION INSURANCE

I am not recommending any of these, but they are a good place to begin finding out about the costs and availability of acquiring a policy. You probably should make initial contact once you have locked your written script and before you finish post-production. It would be an expensive mistake to put material in that the E&O attorney says they cannot cover.

http://www.filmins.com/programs/errors-omissions-insurance.htm

https://www.techinsurance.com/errors-and-omissions-insurance/

http://www.dewittstern.com/content.asp?pageID=56

ASSIGNMENT THREE

Make a checklist of all the clearances you should investigate and possibly clear for a clip from a 1980 domestic feature-length film.

Do the same exercise for a short film produced by a major studio in 1930.

Take your show premise and create a list of geographic and media markets that you will have to clear for anticipated sales.

PART FOUR

HOW TO LOVE ARCHIVAL MATERIAL

CHAPTER 28

MAKING MONEY FROM YOUR OWN STOCK FOOTAGE

FIGURE 28.1. Hollywood party celebrating selling stock footage and making a lot of money. James Forsher collection.

🍃 INTRODUCTION

How do you know if you have archival material worth anything? Here are a few questions you can ask yourself.

Do you have any "one-of-a-kind" material?

If you have any footage that is unique, you might have archival material worth selling. This is material that nobody else has. Original works by an artist? Photographs that are one-of-a-kind shots? Home movies that captured a special time and place? These could all be worth licensing out.

Even though you might not consider it important, remember that in the world of archival-asset purchasers, someone may be doing a film that needs just what you—and only you—have.

Historic Events?

Do you have material that reflects important milestones in history? You might have access to a doll collection, your family's 8mm film collection or your old camcorder videos shot during school. These have all captured a time, a place and possibly a tie to important events.

Events like 9/11 were documented by many people. No matter how many people shot images of that horrific day, all that footage is valuable and should find a home at an archival management company.

Beauty Shots?

There is a constant demand for "beauty shots." These are typically the wonderful majestic images of nature, cities, space, etc. With the increase in quality of both video and still cameras (as well as smartphones), the number of people who can capture these images has grown. If your material has a "wow" factor, then you can merchandise it.

❧ MAYBE I HAVE SOME INTERESTING ARCHIVAL MATERIAL. WHAT DO I DO NEXT?

If you said yes to any of the above questions, you probably have something worth offering. So what do you do? Here are a few options to monetize what you have.

ADOBE PREMIERE PRO

Adobe has created a world of acquiring and licensing stock footage directly through their editing software, Adobe Premiere Pro. The idea is pretty straightforward; you can input the material directly into the file folders in Adobe Premiere Pro and then indicate that you want to make the footage available for licensing as royalty-free footage.

Royalty-free footage means that the buyer gets the footage for a flat price with no limits on time or territory. Many archives now offer this footage—usually material that can be found at several archives and is not one-of-a-kind.

For more information, go to: https://helpx.adobe.com/stock/how-to/adobe-stock-video-footage.html

FIND AN ARCHIVE TO REPRESENT YOUR MATERIAL

You can also try to find an appropriate archive to represent your material. There are archives that specialize in footage, music, still photographs and art. Each of these often have specialties, including sports, nature, war and Hollywood.

I suggest you go through a site like www.footage.net and review different archives. When you find one that has footage similar to what you want to sell, contact them and see if they want to represent your material.

❧ REPRESENT YOURSELF OR ORGANIZE A COLLECTIVE

In this world of one-click searches, you have the option of representing yourself and keeping all the money you get from a sale.

My suggestion is that unless you have hundreds if not thousands of films, you team up with other filmmakers and create a collective. The cost for running an archive includes marketing, online access, storage and sales. It is much easier for several people to share the burden.

You will have a much better chance of succeeding if you have a "niche" in the world of archival material. You will see that many archival houses exist. Many share similar material. They are spending hundreds of thousands of dollars marketing their material. What will set your archive apart is saying that you have very special material. It may be of interest to only three percent of the total marketplace, but nowadays that is enough to stay in business.

❧ SUMMARY

Your personal archival holdings will most likely never make you rich, but they are an asset. Spend a few hours organizing and digitizing your assets. Find the appropriate way to sell them and for the foreseeable future you will have a few hundred—if not a few thousand—dollars coming in each year.

CHAPTER 29

THE REAL SEARCH BEGINS

After spending nearly thirty years of teaching film production and over forty years of producing films and television shows, I have found two truths.

1. Film projects are much more interesting when you have the assets to bring the story to life. Films suffer when you repeat the same photos five times, keep coming back to the same close-up

FIGURE 29.1. Public domain Beatles. Universal Newsreel coverage of the Fab 4 arrival in the United States during the mid-1960s. Footagesource.com

and stay on an interview subject too long because you don't have enough material to cover the shot.

2. Filmmakers that learn their trade in school never hear about how archival assets make a show richer. I don't know why, but my theory is that most film editing instructors didn't learn how to integrate archival material into a shot and students don't have a strong historic visual sense. They have a tough time looking at an image and deciding what period of time it came from or what region of the world it was shot in. The easiest solution is not to use it.

My hope is by the time you read this, you have realized that an immense amount of material exists to help you tell your story, whether it is a montage in a feature to establish a time and place, a newsreel for an archive, or works of art tied to a virtual reality show on a famous painter.

I hope you have gotten over the stereotype of archival assets being just grainy black-and-white footage and that you now realize they can be any asset that was shot as recently as an hour ago and will help make your program the best work possible.

The previous twenty-eight chapters have taken you through the process of figuring out what is out there, who owns it and how to secure it. Now it is up to you to choose from a nearly unlimited amount of material that, when chosen carefully, will make your program truly extra-ordinary.

❦ KEEP IN TOUCH

All readers of this book are invited to go to www.footagesource.com and sign up for the newsletter as well as join our blog community. I will continuously share the archival sources and experiences you all put on the blog as well as the latest information I uncover in the fabulous world of archival material hunting.

⟿ *SPOTLIGHT ON* . . .

FOUND FOOTAGE EXERCISES

Many of you may want to try using archival material but don't have a project in mind. If you want to affordably produce a story, we are offering Found Footage Workbooks that give you some archival footage and a set of instructions on how to cut the archival material into a contemporary story. Go to www.footagesource.com for a list of topics available.

ASSIGNMENT FOUR

Your goal is to figure out if you have material in your own collection that can be exploited.

1. Make an Excel spreadsheet with the following columns:

    Title • Reel # • Length • Description • Location • Notes • Audience

2. Add all of your material. Do not limit yourself. Put everything down.

3. Once you are done, review the audience portion and see how many films you have that others might be interested in. Audience interest may mean nature shows, war films, establishing shots, science fiction . . . anything that you can describe to a film archive that lets them know that your film has commercial potential.

ABOUT THE AUTHOR

JAMES FORSHER is a retired associate professor in Communication, having taught at California State University, East Bay, Seattle University, Temple University and Florida State University. He has served as a Fulbright Specialist at Klagenfurt University in 2015 and the University of Vienna in 2018. His academic background is a blend of an interest in American cultural institutions and communication studies, which he has examined both in written works and as a television producer.

His television programs include the twenty-six part *Hollywood Chronicles* for the Discovery Channel (1990), the eight-part *Changing Culture of the Workplace* (1995), *The Hollywood Censorship Wars* for the Arts & Entertainment Network (1994), *Lost Warriors* for PBS (1998) and the thirteen-part *The 1960s* for Encore! Feature-length specials include *Hollywood Uncensored* and *Hollywood Ghost Stories* (which have aired on such systems as Cinemax and The Movie Channel). He recently produced the documentary *Roddenberry's Trek* and developed and narrated the 2017 ORF/Langbein production of *Elvis Und Das Madschen Aus Wien* (*Elvis and the Girl From Vienna*). Dr. Forsher wrote *The Community of Cinema: How Cinema and Spectacle Transformed the American Downtown* (Praeger, 2002).

He has served as a consultant for a number of organizations, including ABC News and PBS Marketplace. He also was a producer of visual content for Pearson as well as Allyn & Bacon publishers.

One tremendous resource of James Forsher is his in-house archive that has several thousand titles. For nearly thirty years the archive has been a resource for hundreds of documentaries, rock videos and television commercial producers. The archive is rich in Americana and entertainment-related footage that spans the era before the turn of the century through the 1990s.

Dr. Forsher received his PhD in Urban and Regional Planning from the University of Southern California with an emphasis in community studies and information technologies.

You may contact James Forsher though this website: http://www.stockfootagethebook.com

THE WRITER'S JOURNEY
3RD EDITION

MYTHIC STRUCTURE FOR WRITERS

CHRISTOPHER VOGLER

BEST SELLER
OVER 170,000 COPIES SOLD!

See why this book has become an international best seller and a true classic. *The Writer's Journey* explores the powerful relationship between mythology and storytelling in a clear, concise style that's made it required reading for movie executives, screenwriters, playwrights, scholars, and fans of pop culture all over the world.

Both fiction and nonfiction writers will discover a set of useful myth-inspired storytelling paradigms (i.e., "The Hero's Journey") and step-by-step guidelines to plot and character development. Based on the work of Joseph Campbell, *The Writer's Journey* is a must for all writers interested in further developing their craft.

The updated and revised third edition provides new insights and observations from Vogler's ongoing work on mythology's influence on stories, movies, and man himself.

"This book is like having the smartest person in the story meeting come home with you and whisper what to do in your ear as you write a screenplay. Insight for insight, step for step, Chris Vogler takes us through the process of connecting theme to story and making a script come alive."
　　　　－ Lynda Obst, Producer, *Sleepless in Seattle, How to Lose a Guy in 10 Days;*
　　　　　Author, *Hello, He Lied*

"This is a book about the stories we write, and perhaps more importantly, the stories we live. It is the most influential work I have yet encountered on the art, nature, and the very purpose of storytelling."
　　　　－ Bruce Joel Rubin, Screenwriter, *Stuart Little 2, Deep Impact,*
　　　　　Ghost, Jacob's Ladder

CHRISTOPHER VOGLER is a veteran story consultant for major Hollywood film companies and a respected teacher of filmmakers and writers around the globe. He has influenced the stories of movies from *The Lion King* to *Fight Club* to *The Thin Red Line* and most recently wrote the first installment of *Ravenskull*, a Japanese-style manga or graphic novel. He is the executive producer of the feature film *P.S. Your Cat is Dead* and writer of the animated feature *Jester Till*.

$27.95 · 300 PAGES · ORDER NUMBER 76RLS · ISBN: 193290736x

MAKING IT BIG IN SHORTS
– 3RD EDITION
THE ULTIMATE FILMMAKER'S GUIDE TO SHORT FILMS

KIM ADELMAN

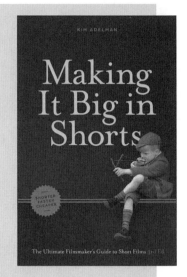

Making a short is something to be proud of. Just ask Jack Nicholson. The hard part is making a good short. Everyone makes shorts – famous directors, movie stars, entertainment-industry professionals, feature filmmakers, students, and regular folk from all over the world.

Each year 8,000+ short films compete to fill 60 slots at the Sundance Film Festival. On an average day, 792 film and video projects vie for funding on Kickstarter. And every minute 300 hours of video are uploaded to YouTube.

In this competitive environment, a short filmmaker can no longer invest time, money, and dreams of glory in the theory that "if you build it, they will come." The challenge is making the right kind of short: one that will make a splash.

Covering the nuts-and-bolts of production while stressing the importance of artistic expression, this invaluable handbook shows a first-time filmmaker how to make a buzz-worthy little film that could launch a lucrative Hollywood career.

Packed with over 75 photos and insider advice from dozens of high-profile professionals, including Sundance and Tribeca festival programmers and Academy Award® winners and nominees, *Making It Big in Shorts* puts the emphasis on making films shorter, faster, and cheaper.

"Forget film school; this book is all you need! Adelman's spot-on advice comes from years in the trenches of indie filmmaking; her expertise breaks down the process of making your film and getting it seen."

—Andrea Richards, author, *Girl Director: A How-To Guide for the First Time, Flat-Broke Film* and *Video Maker*

KIM ADELMAN currently teaches Low-Budget Filmmaking at UCLA Extension. She was honored as Instructor of the Year in 2014 and won the UCLA Extension Distinguished Instructor Award in 2016. She lectures annually at the USC School of Cinematic Arts' Career Week. She has conducted filmmaking workshops across the United States, Canada, and New Zealand.

$16.95 · 156 PAGES · ORDER #240RLS · ISBN 9781615932566

FILMMAKING FOR CHANGE:
MAKE FILMS THAT TRANSFORM THE WORLD, 2ND EDITION

JON FITZGERALD

Grab a camera! Make a difference! Whether you are an experienced filmmaker looking to expose social wrongs or someone who has never made a movie but wants to, this is the book for you.

Recognizing that film is the most powerful form of political activism, you will learn the keys to *Filmmaking for Change*, from story ideas to production, film festivals and distribution.

Industry veteran Jon Fitzgerald has developed a new manual for making socially activist films on a low budget, from concept development through production, from marketing through distribution.

In straightforward sections, with descriptive breakdowns for each category, the book presents a new paradigm for social-impact filmmaking in the modern age — including case studies on numerous films and advice from industry professionals on each topic.

"Films can have a profound impact . . . and truly create everlasting, positive change. This book will help you create a blueprint for empowering action."

> —Morgan Spurlock, Academy Award nominated filmmaker:
> *Super Size Me*

With a degree in Film Studies from the University of California at Santa Barbara, JON FITZGERALD directed his first film in 1994, and then cofounded the Slamdance Film Festival in 1995 and was the Executive Director for the next two years before becoming the Festival Director at the American Film Institute (1997–1999) and then the Santa Barbara and Abu Dhabi International Film Festivals. In 2003, he formed Right Angle Studios, a consulting firm that provided services to numerous film festivals and indie filmmakers. In 2009, Fitzgerald transitioned back into production, developing socially relevant films through Cause Pictures (*The Back Nine, Dance of Liberation, The Highest Pass, The Milky Way, Warrior One*). In 2015, Fitzgerald launched Causecinema.com as a guide to the best of social impact films. The website provides a filter to quality social impact films, supported by podcasts, showcases, and web series, while increasing awareness and donations to related causes around the world.

$26.95 · 270 PAGES · ORDER #250RLS · ISBN 9781615932771

THE MYTH OF MWP

In a dark time, a light bringer came along, leading the curious and the frustrated to clarity and empowerment. It took the well-guarded secrets out of the hands of the few and made them available to all. It spread a spirit of openness and creative freedom, and built a storehouse of knowledge dedicated to the betterment of the arts.

The essence of the Michael Wiese Productions (MWP) is empowering people who have the burning desire to express themselves creatively. We help them realize their dreams by putting the tools in their hands. We demystify the sometimes secretive worlds of screenwriting, directing, acting, producing, film financing, and other media crafts.

By doing so, we hope to bring forth a realization of 'conscious media' which we define as being positively charged, emphasizing hope and affirming positive values like trust, cooperation, self-empowerment, freedom, and love. Grounded in the deep roots of myth, it aims to be healing both for those who make the art and those who encounter it. It hopes to be transformative for people, opening doors to new possibilities and pulling back veils to reveal hidden worlds.

MWP has built a storehouse of knowledge unequaled in the world, for no other publisher has so many titles on the media arts. Please visit www.mwp.com where you will find many free resources and a 25% discount on our books. Sign up and become part of the wider creative community!

Onward and upward,

Michael Wiese
Publisher/Filmmaker